CAPITALISM VERSUS SOCIALISM:
THE GREAT SELIGMAN-NEARING DEBATE OF 1921

RELATED TITLES FROM ANTIC PRESS

Charles T. Sprading, *The Laconics of Liberty*

∼

Visit us at www.AnticPress.com

Capitalism

versus

Socialism

The Great Seligman-Nearing Debate of 1921

Rob Weir

Antic Press
Dover, New Hampshire

Copyright © 2020 by Rob Weir.

International Standard Book Number: 978-1-7338971-3-6 (pb)

Portions based on the text of A Public Debate "Capitalism vs. Socialism," copyright 1921, The Fine Arts Guild, Inc.

All rights reserved. No part of this publication may be reproduced, distributed or transmitted in any form or by any means, including photocopying, recording, or other electronic or mechanical methods, without the prior written permission of the publisher, except in the case of brief quotations embodied in critical reviews and certain other noncommercial uses permitted by copyright law.

Antic Press
106 Court St.
Dover, NH 03820

www.anticpress.com

Capitalism Versus Socialism: The Great Seligman-Nearing Debate of 1921/ Rob Weir. —1st ed.

Dedication

To Diane, my ever-ready debate partner, on any topic, at any time, from first light, to the last.

Contents

Dedication v

Resolution... ix

Preface... xi

Introduction xv

Editorial Notes... xxv

Moderator Introduction (Villard) 1

Analysis of Introduction.. 7

Affirmative (Seligman) 9

Analysis of Affirmative 25

Negative (Nearing) 29

Analysis of Negative 43

Affirmative Rebuttal (Seligman).. 47

Analysis of Affirmative Rebuttal... 57

Negative Rebuttal (Nearing) 59

Analysis of Negative Rebuttal 69

Affirmative Conclusion (Seligman) 73

Analysis of Affirmative Conclusion 79

Negative Conclusion (Nearing) 81

Analysis of Negative Conclusion 85

Who Won the Debate? 87

Reactions and Recollections 89

What did Mises see? 93

Appendix A 95

Appendix B 101

Appendix C 103

Appendix D 109

About the Author 115

Resolution

That Capitalism has more to offer to the workers of the United States than has Socialism.

The Socialist Review, January 1921, back cover.

Preface

I was recently reading Ludwig von Mises's 1927 book, *Liberalism*,[1] a powerful argument for the virtues of a free society, written at a time when Europe stood on the edge of an abyss, staring into the darkness of authoritarianism, soon to take its fateful plunge. In an appendix to that book, "On the literature of liberalism," Mises listed works that he considered to be "the most important literature" on the subject. Famous works were included, such as the classic texts of Locke, Mill, and Bastiat. But Mises also listed more obscure, contemporary titles. What caught my eye was a note in the section on American liberal writings where Mises wrote:

> Also instructive (*lehrreich*) is the record of the public debate held in New York on January 23, 1921, between E.R.A. Seligman and Scott Nearing on the topic: "That capitalism has more to offer to the workers of the United States than has socialism."

---

[1] The original Germany title was *Liberalismus*. The first U.S. edition (1962, Ralph Raico, translator) was called *The Free and Prosperous Commonwealth*, avoiding the word "liberal" in the title since the term had a Leftist connotation in America since the early 20th century.

I tracked down a transcript of the debate, published by the Fine Arts Guild in 1921, and long since out of print. I found it to be a pleasant and instructive short book, and one that deserves to be better known to audiences today.

Why? First, the question of capitalism versus socialism has returned to the headlines. It is part of our contemporary debate now more than any time in recent memory. We recently had a self-avowed socialist running for president. Three members of Congress are members of the Democratic Socialists of America,[2] with many more holding state and local offices.

Despite the earnest hope and belief that the story of socialism was closed with the collapse of the Soviet Union and her puppet states in Eastern Europe, the lessons from this painful period in our history were not indelibly encoded into our DNA. Each new generation is charmed anew by the enticing promises of socialism. Each generation must learn for itself. We can only hope the education, in this round, is far less dramatic than the last. Debates, whether as a live event,[3] or in written

---

[2] Danny K. Davis (Illinois), Alexandria Ocasio-Cortez (New York), and Rashida Tlaib (Michigan).

[3] On March 5, 2019 the Soho Forum in New York City held a debate on the resolution, "Socialism is preferable to capitalism as an economic system that promotes freedom, equality, and prosperity," where Richard Wolff argued the affirmative and Gene Epstein the negative. Epstein won this Oxford-style debate, bringing more of the audience over to his position.

form, remain a popular and effective way of educating the public about such issues.

Second, this debate helps us better understand Mises and his contributions. Understanding the state of liberalism (such as it was) in America in the 1920s, and the best arguments that could be rallied to its defense, shows the comparative brilliance of the arguments that Mises and Hayek and others of the Austrian School would soon be making. Knowing more about what Mises saw as "instructive" in the writings of his early contemporaries helps us better understand his thinking in these formative years.

It is for these two reasons that I am bringing this edition to publication, and why I commend it to your attention.

Rob Weir
Dover, New Hampshire.
December 2020

S.S
S4657de

DEBATE *between*
Prof. E. R. A. SELIGMAN, *Affirmative*
Head of the Department of Economics, Columbia University

and

Prof. SCOTT NEARING, *Negative*
Rand School of Social Science

Oswald Garrison Villard,
Editor of "THE NATION"

Subject

Resolved: That Capitalism has more to offer to the workers of the United States than has Socialism.

LEXINGTON THEATRE
NEW YORK CITY
JANUARY 23, 1921

UNDER THE AUSPICES OF
The Fine Arts Guild, Inc.
27 West 8th Street
New York City

VERBATIM REPORT
BY
The Convention Reporting Co.
NEW YORK CITY

Title page of the original 1921 transcription.

Introduction

The Setting

Sunday, January 23, 1921, midtown Manhattan, the Lexington Theater.[4] It was a good day to watch a fight. A packed audience attended the sold-out event. Most were from New York, but there was also a sizable contingent who traveled in from Boston and Philadelphia. An estimated 3,500 were in the theater, while others sought out tickets, at a stiff markup, from hawkers on the sidewalk.

Was this a boxing match? A wrestling bout? An exhibition of martial arts? No, this was to be a battle between two economics professors, a three-round debate on a weighty topic on everyone's mind: capitalism versus socialism.

Before getting into the debate itself, it is worth a brief diversion to discuss the political climate at the time, in the United States and abroad, in order to understand why this debate garnered such interest.

---

[4] The Lexington Theater, midtown Manhattan, 571 Lexington Avenue, was originally built as an opera house by Oscar Hammerstein I, the grandfather of the famed Broadway lyricist, Oscar Hammerstein II.

Revolution!

Revolution was in the air after the Great War. Germany's loss precipitated a constitutional crisis there—the November Revolution of 1918—triggering revolts and a series of short-lived socialist republics in Bavaria, Bremen, and Saxony. Hungary was rocked by a series of revolutions between 1918 and 1920. The Irish Easter Rising of 1916 led to an Irish War of Independence in 1919. Egypt revolted against the British that same year. Mongolia revolted to expel the White Russian forces, and Finland revolted to expel the Reds. And, of course, there was the mother of all revolutions: the Bolshevik revolution in Russia and the resulting Russian Civil War.

Americans were jittery, worried that revolution would be imported to our shores. This was the time of the Red Scare.

In 1919 Italian anarchists, followers of Luigi Galleani, sent several dozen mail bombs to prominent politicians, journalists, and industrialists. This was answered by the Palmer Raids of January 1920. Wilson's Justice Department rounded up 10,000 foreigners with suspected radical ties. Many of the arrested were deported. The unrest continued. In September 1920 Wall Street was bombed. Thirty-eight died.

Would revolution come to the United States as it had in Europe? There was ample reason for discontent. The post-war economy was in rough shape, with declining GDP, price deflation, and high unemployment.[5] People were suffering. And let's not forget the Spanish Flu epidemic, the fourth wave of which hit New York City in the spring of 1920.

It would be an exaggeration to say the country was on the brink, but unlike today, where socialism can be debated with some degree of academic detachment, in the years immediately following Word War I there was a very real sense of vulnerability, a fear that America could be next.

It's (now) Debatable

A few years earlier, during the war, giving socialism a platform in a debate would have been impossible. Wilson's draconian Espionage and Sedition Acts[6] stifled political discourse. In fact, one of the participants in our debate, Scott Nearing, had been arrested and tried under these laws for writing a pamphlet critical of the war. But by 1921, the Red Scare was waning. A new president had been elected, Warren Harding, who

---

[5] Curiously, the Depression of 1920-21 rather quickly resolved itself without government intervention. See Thomas E. Woods Jr., "The Forgotten Depression of 1920" (https://mises.org/library/forgotten-depression-1920 : accessed 1 Dec. 2020); also, James Grant, T*he Forgotten Depression: 1921: The Crash That Cured Itself* (Simon & Schuster, 2014).

[6] The Espionage Act of 1917, among other things, outlawed attempts to "willfully obstruct the recruiting or enlistment service of the United States." The Sedition Act of 1918 essentially criminalized opposing the war.

promised a "return to normalcy." A debate, such as this, with two sides presenting their views, was now palatable to authorities. And it appears that there was pent up demand.

The Resolution

The resolution of the debate, sponsored by the Fine Arts Guild, was: "That Capitalism has more to offer to the workers of the United States than has Socialism."

For the Affirmative: E.R.A. Seligman

Taking the affirmative on the resolution was Professor Edwin R.A. Seligman (1861-1939). Seligman was born in New York City, the son of Joseph Seligman, a Jewish merchant who emigrated to the U.S. and later founded, with his brothers, the prominent investment banking firm of J. & W. Seligman.

Edwin grew up in a prosperous home and was given every opportunity to develop his faculties. His private tutor was Horatio Alger,[7] who lived in their home until 1876. Seligman soon was noted for facility with languages, learning Latin, Greek, German, French, Italian, Spanish, and later Dutch and Russian. Declining to follow his father into banking, Edwin entered Columbia

---

[7] Alger is best remembered today for his Gilded Age "rags-to-riches" novels.

at 14, graduating in four years, and then going abroad for further studies.[8]

In Germany and France, Seligman was steeped in the German Historical School of economics. However, according to one account, his mature views were not limited to that perspective:

> His sojourn in Europe had a remarkable effect on him in two directions. In the first place, he was deeply struck by the teaching of Wagner in Berlin and the influence of the German historical school. He realised, however, that its advancement had not been one without grave errors and many sacrifices. It had led to a considerable degree of stagnation in German economics because of its isolation from the movement of economic thought in other countries. The criticism and later the complete rejection of classical doctrines, he realised, barred German economists from taking an interest in the refinements upon classical theory produced by foreign scholars. The violent polemics between Schmoller and

---

[8] Wesley C. Mitchell, "Edwin Robert Anderson Seligman, 1861-1939," *American Economic Review*, Vol. 29, No. 4 (Dec. 1939), pp. 911-913.

Menger[9] did not turn Seligman away, as it did many German economists, from marginalist economics, which has been more popular than any other school of economics, and he was an outstanding example of his time, certainly in the United States, that every economic theorist should be something of a historian and every student of the development of economic institutions must be something of a theorist.[10]

Returning to Columbia in 1882 Seligman studied political science and law (economics was not yet a distinct academic field of study) and received a Ph.D and LL.B. In 1885 he co-founded the American Economic Association. He specialized in public finance, particularly taxation, and was a key proponent of the progressive income tax.

At the time of the 1921 debate, Seligman was 60 years old and chair of the Department of Economics at Columbia.

---

[9] The *Methodenstreit* (methodological fight) was a debate in economics in the 1880s between the German Historical School, represented by Gustav von Schmoller, and what would later be called the Austrian School, represented by Carl Menger. The question was whether economic knowledge comes from statistical examination of historical evidence (German Historical School), or whether knowledge can come from logical argumentation from axiomatic principles (the Austrian School).
[10] G. Findlay Shirras, "Obituary: Edwin Robert Anderson Seligman (1861-1939)," *Economic Journal*, Vol. 49, No. 195 (Sep. 1939), pp. 577-589.

For the Negative: Scott Nearing

Scott Nearing (1883-1983) was born in coal country, in Tiago County, Pennsylvania, the son of a stockbroker. He studied oratory at Temple University, and economics at the Wharton School at the University of Pennsylvania, where he received a Ph.D. in Economics in 1909, followed by a professorship. This ended, however, in 1915 when his advocacy of radical causes led to his dismissal, an action widely condemned at the time as an attack on academic freedom.

Nearing then taught at Toledo University, where in 1917 he was dismissed for his anti-war speeches. Undeterred, he continued to speak and write against the war. One pamphlet, "The Great Madness: A Victory for the American Plutocracy," led to his indictment under Wilson's Espionage Act. In the trial, the charges against Nearing were eventually dropped, but two charges against his publisher resulted in a modest fine.

Nearing finally found security teaching at a school that welcomed his radical perspective. He taught at the Rand School of Social Science in New York City, a school for activists run by the Socialist Party of America.

In later life (he lived to the age of 100), Nearing was an advocate for pacifism, vegetarianism, and simple living. His final years were spent on a farm in Maine.

At the time of our debate, Scott Nearing was an affirmed socialist, a radical economist, and Seligman's junior by 25 years.

The Moderator: Oswald Garrison Villard

The chairman of the debate was Oswald Garrison Villard (1872-1949), grandson of the famous abolitionist, William Lloyd Garrison. Villard studied American History (Harvard '93), but then turned from academia to activism and journalism.

Villard was a co-founder of the American Anti-Imperialist League and the NAACP. He also was the editor and owner of "The Nation," a progressive weekly.

Although at the time of the debate Villard had progressive leanings, his noninterventionist leanings, as well as concerns that the New Deal was a prelude to fascism, led him later to oppose F.D.R. We might fairly consider Villard to be a member of the Old Right.

The Format

The debate lasted three hours. After an introduction by Villard each side was given an opportunity for an introduction, with the affirmative side (Seligman) going first. After introductions, each side was allowed a rebuttal. The debate ended with each side giving concluding remarks, with Nearing getting the last word.

Not Their First Encounter

Seligman and Nearing had previously clashed in an acrimonious debate on March 17, 1917 at the Academy of Music in Brooklyn on the question, "Have our universities academic freedom?" Nearing, arguing the negative, asserted that professors were teaching what they did not believe to be true, and that they were essentially prostitutes. Seligman, indignant at these comments, jumped to his feet and declared:

> I want to publicly state that I will have nothing to do with any man who would arraign his colleagues as Professor Nearing has arraigned them tonight. And furthermore, any professor who makes such a statement has no right to demand recognition in any university in this country.

Newspaper coverage of this earlier debate can be found in Appendices A and B.

Avoidance of Presentism

It is difficult for us today to read this debate from the perspective of a 1921 audience. We are informed by an additional century of history where these ideas battled each other throughout the world. We know what happened in the Soviet Union. We know about the Great Depression. We know about Word War II.

Reading this debate is like reading a debate on cruise liner safety argued in 1911, the year before the R.M.S. *Titanic* met its fate.

When reading this debate, it is important to avoid "presentism" and to clearly segregate in our minds the observations that might have been made in 1921, based on information known at that time, from those critiques that rely on information known only later. The socialist of 1921 might be guilty of many follies, but not knowing about Stalin, Mao, or Pol Pot are not fairly counted among them, given that none of these men were yet in power. American socialists of 1921 are also not to be blamed for lack of familiarity with theoretical critiques, such as the "economic calculation problem," available at the time only in German publications.[11]

---

[11] Mises first published this critique in a 1920 article, "Die Wirtschaftsrechnung im sozialistischen Gemeinwesen" in *Archiv für Sozialwissenschaft und Sozialpolitik*.

Editorial Notes

The original published transcription of this debate, based on a stenographic copy, appears to have been hastily prepared and contains many misspellings and other typographical errors which I have silently corrected.

The original spoken debate had no intrinsic punctuation or paragraph breaks. Rather than accept, without question, the choices of the original publisher, I have amended the text where I believed clarity and readability would benefit, e.g., favoring shorter paragraphs and a more modern approach to punctuation and capitalization.

Finally, I have added footnotes to illuminate historical references which an audience of 1921 might have understood, but which might be obscure to a modern reader.

Announcement!

If you want announcements of interesting lectures and debates send your name to

THE FINE ARTS GUILD, Inc.
27 West Eighth Street
New York

If you live out-of-town and desire to arrange interesting lectures and debates on vital subjects for groups, clubs, forums or organizations, communicate with

THE FINE ARTS GUILD, Inc.
27 West Eighth Street
New York

Fine Arts Guild advertisement.

Moderator Introduction (Villard)

A Debate on Capitalism vs. Socialism

It seems to me that the function of a chairman of this debate ought to partake of the character of a refereeship. I believe that you would be most pleased if I were to simply make the debaters come forward, shake hands, and then fall to, I standing by with my watch in hand to take the time. In fact, I really cannot see why the chairman should say anything on this occasion. But I suppose I was chosen for this sporting event because I am a middle-of-the-roader between the two. I am not a socialist, and yet I am not one who believes that socialists are wild beasts to be excluded from polite society and legislatures because we do not like their point of view on matters economic and social.

I grew up in the tradition of the Manchester school[12] of laissez-faire and I still believe that if human nature were what it ought to be, the doctrines of this school would be the ones to be followed. But I am open-minded enough to see that, whether we like socialism or do not, the experiment is going to be tried in large sections of the Earth.

---

[12] Centered in Manchester, England, the Manchester School pushed for free trade reforms. The Anti-Corn Law League (1838) was its most important institution, and men like Richard Cobden and John Bright were its most prominent leaders.

I was very much struck by the fact that when I returned from Europe, a few months after the Armistice,[13] there were few people whom I met who would believe that I had seen the Red Flag flying over as many public buildings as I saw others that did not have it. It seemed to make Americans very angry to tell them that their troops had been the decisive factor in creating twenty-three socialist republics in Germany alone, to say nothing of the other central European republics.

When I returned, I found New York City forbidding the hoisting or carrying of the Red Flag, and, as you know, there exists the greatest confusion in the minds of public men and editors in America as to what constitutes socialism. To most of our leader-writers there is no difference whatever between the socialism of the right, the socialism of the left, Bolshevism, communism, and anarchism. They are all anathema to the American businessman, who lumps them together. Hence, any such occasion as this is heartily to be welcomed, not only for its educational value but because it indicates a return to our habitual American policy of talking things out on their merits, fairly and openly. Lately, the idea has been to lynch the socialist first and discuss matters with him afterwards.

We are having additional evidence of this intolerance of new ideas in the refusal of the American Legion in

---

[13] November 11, 1919.

Kansas to allow the Nonpartisan League's[14] organizers to talk to the farmers of that state about their proposals for the farmers' economic freedom. How inconsistent we are in these matters appears further from the fact that at the very moment that the socialist legislators were being thrown out of the legislature at Albany,[15] the then governor of the state, Alfred Smith,[16] solemnly proposed no less than nine ultra-radical or socialistic laws, including such things as the ownership, development, and operation of all water powers by the state, maternity insurance, the municipal operation of all public utilities, the taking over of the medical and nursing professions to the extent of supplying doctors and nurses to rural communities now destitute of such aid, the declaration that production and distribution of milk are a public utility subject to the control of the state in all details, and state-owned and operated grain elevators in three cities, precisely after the manner of the Nonpartisan League plans in North Dakota.

---

[14] The Nonpartisan League (NPL), led by a socialist organizer, Arthur C. Townley, promoted state ownership and control of agriculture, mainly in in North Dakota.

[15] In April 1920, five state legislatures were expelled from the New York Assembly for disloyalty to the United States and membership in the Socialist Party of America. All five ran, and were re-elected, to their seats in September of that year, after which they were expelled again. Two of them then ran again in the November election and were re-re-elected. Further attempts to expel them failed.

[16] Alfred E. Smith (1873-1944) was a Progressive politician, serving four terms as New York governor. He also was the presidential nominee for the Democrats in 1928.

I have long thought that "Al" Smith was a wonderful man, but I do not know of anything in his career that is more wonderful than the fact that he got away with these proposals without even being denounced as a socialist by the New York Times. Of course, he did not get what he asked, but the point is that if the governor of North Dakota were to come out tomorrow and demand these things, the New York Times would shriek with anger and declare that Bolshevizing of America was at hand. The so-called socialistic experiments of North Dakota can be paralleled in most every state in one field or another, as for instance, in the cotton warehouses in New Orleans and the grain elevators now being erected in New York State. While North Dakota's proposal to issue bonds for home-building[17] has led to the rejection of their 6.5 million bond issue by New York and Boston bankers, many eminent and conservative senators are feeling that here in the East, the states, and even the federal government, will have to go into the housing business.

All of which, I think, proves my case that the socialistic experiment, in greater or less degree, is going to be undertaken by the world. In the ardent hope that it may produce a better world than we have been living in, my plea today is, as I have said, not for socialism, but for a careful examination of this and all other proposals for the betterment of the race which is so badly off, that, for

---

[17] North Dakota's 1919 Home-Building Act allowed the state to issue bonds, the proceeds to be used to fund home-building.

all we know, civilization may not recover from the shock of this war.

I am sure that I cannot define the position which the non-socialist public ought to take towards this question better than by reading to you an extract from an editorial which appeared about ten years ago in the columns of the New York Nation from the pen of its gifted and noble-spirited editor of that day, the late Hammond Lamont.[18] It is as follows:

> Convinced though we are that the reasoning of the socialists is fallacious, we incline to the belief that a socialist agitation may in the long run prove beneficial to this country. We were opposed to the free coinage of silver, and yet we are convinced that the two great political campaigns in which that subject was treated so fully in the press and on the platform were extremely valuable in their educational effect. Thousands, nay, millions, of men and women who had grown up without the slightest notion of economics in general and finance in particular, became fairly well versed in the topic; they were made more intelligent and better citizens; and in the end they sustained the principle of sound money.

---

[18] Hammond Lamont (1864-1909) was the third editor of Nation, coming after Wendell Philips Garrison (Oswald Garrison Villard's uncle) and before Paul Elmer More.

In like manner socialism may be the means of widening intellectual horizons; it may lay before Americans a new view of some of the larger questions of life, far larger than the petty tenets of trades-unionism. It may set us to thinking; and the salvation of a republic depends upon the efforts of its citizens to think seriously about its affairs. For one thing, socialism is eminently a peace movement; it is steadily opposed to militarism; and it will thus help us to see more clearly the silliness of the huge naval and military expenditures in which we seem bound to rival the groaning nations of Europe. And as for other questions, we cannot believe that error will permanently prevail over truth. We are confident that individualism, in its main features, is the policy which has formed and which must preserve our institutions. But if we conservatives are mistaken, we cannot but welcome a discussion which shall open our eyes and set us right. Our attitude toward this topic, as towards any other which touches the vitals of our nation, must be that of readiness to defend our faith in open forum, to meet and conquer with reason.

Analysis of Introduction

What can we say of the chairman, Mr. Villard, and his introduction of the debate? His argument, in the large, is that there is a lot of fear of socialism in America, that it has become a bogeyman of sorts, that it cannot be discussed in some parts of the country. Nevertheless, socialist ideas, when they are brought up without using that term, are soberly considered. Since state government in the United States has a great deal of independence, experiments with socialism are bound to happen there. We should, Villard argues, allow and encourage such tinkering, with the confidence that truth will win out in the end and we will all be the better for the experience.

Villard is exhibiting the thematic Progressive attitude, that society is infinitely malleable and improvable, and if we could just get the right, smart people together in the room, and give them the power to make substantive changes, then good things would come about. That is how progress happens. We see it all around us, in the works of science, engineering, and industry.

However, note that Professor Seligman is also a Progressive and has a similar attitude. So, we should not expect to hear in this debate a Burkean, conservative argument based on moderation, respect for existing traditions, institutions, and norms. As we will see,

Seligman's approach is instead based on tinkering with and improving capitalism itself, what he will refer to as "progressive capitalism."

Affirmative (Seligman)

Mr. Chairman, Ladies and Gentlemen: In beginning a debate of this magnitude, it is pertinent to inquire what the words mean. What do we really understand by capitalism and what by socialism? Unless we are clear about that, we are wandering in a maze of uncertainty.

Now, by capitalism, I think we may understand that form of industrial organization where the means of production—and by that, I mean (primarily under modern technological conditions) the machine and the funds required to work the machine—are in the control of private individuals.

The difficulty of defining socialism is that while capitalism is an institution, socialism is only a theory, unless indeed we except[19] the sporadic examples that we find in the middle of the 19th century in this country, and unless we also accept the gigantic enterprise that is now being conducted by Soviet Russia.

There are all manner of forms of socialism and socialistic theory. There is the communistic socialism. There is the anarchistic socialism. There is the state socialism. There is the sentimental and scientific socialism. And finally, there is the guild socialism. What is worse, the socialists

---

[19] The original transcription had the word "except" here, and in the next clause, though "accept" seems to be what was intended.

themselves are by no means in agreement. The scientific socialist, the Marxist, scorns the sentimental socialist. The Marxian socialism is supposed to be interpreted by the Menshevik socialist, but the Menshevik is put by the Bolshevik socialist in the ranks of the bourgeoisie. So that you have your choice of the different brands of socialism as a theory.

But as an organization, as an industrial form, all these various forms and kinds of socialism are permeated by one common idea: that is, that the control of the methods of production, that the control of capital (for, of course, socialists like everyone else concede the necessity of capital) that the control of capital shall be in the hands of the group and that there shall be no room for private rent, private interest, or private profits.

Having thus defined those two opposing ideas, the next point that I desire to make is that while there are all forms and kinds of capitalists, just as there are all kinds and mariner of human beings, there are reactionary or stand-pat[20] capitalists and forward-looking, progressive capitalists. While that is true, my contention is that there is only one form of capitalism and that is progressive capitalism. Every form of industrial organization is progressive.

---

[20] "Stand pat" is a term from card games like poker and blackjack, referring to the decision to remain with the cards originally dealt to the player, i.e., to avoid change.

Slavery in the early centuries was very different from slavery in the later centuries. Serfdom at the beginning was very different from serfdom at the end. Feudalism at the inception was quite contrary perhaps in many respects, to feudalism at the end. Capitalism is in the very earliest stages of its development and there are still huge portions of the world which have not yet entered upon capitalism, like parts of China, like Africa, like many other portions of the world. My contention, therefore, is that by capitalism we mean a progressive form of industrial society.

The next point I desire to make is that capitalism must not be misunderstood. Our debate relates to the welfare of the laborer under capitalism. Now, it depends not alone upon the direct results so far as the laborer is concerned, what he gets in the way of food and remuneration for his services, etc., but it depends also upon the indirect results. Therefore, the problem is not simply an analysis of the better distribution of wealth, but it is also the far more important problem of the production of wealth. We must consider the two forms of industrial organization from both these points of view.

And finally, before we proceed to come to close grips with the subject itself, let me call attention to the fact that, while I do not intend to discuss the theories of socialism nor the ideal framework of society as elaborated by Karl Marx, I do wish to point out that among his many fundamental doctrines, two at least and those most germane to our discussion are no longer upheld and maintained by many of the socialists themselves.

The ordinary socialist will say to you that the rich are getting richer and the poor are getting poorer. That is simply putting into common language, the pauperization theory of society as outlined by Karl Marx. We all know however that the facts have given lie to this statement and while it is true that the rich have gotten richer, it is also true that the poor are no longer so poor as they were. This has led no less important socialists than Bernstein[21] in Germany and Tugan Baronowsky[22] in Russia to say, "Let us abandon that argument for socialism."

The other argument which is germane to our discussion is the cataclysm theory of society, the argument of Marx that owing to the accumulation of capital, crises occur every few years, that these crises and panics go from worse to worse until finally they become so overwhelming in their nature that a catastrophic cataclysm of society will occur, and socialism will come in.

Marx wrote in the fifties and sixties, and indeed in the early period of capitalist society, it seemed as if his theory were being borne out by the facts. The panic of 1837 was worse than that of 1818; that of 1857 was still worse: that of 1873, the world-wide crisis, the worst of all. But then,

---

[21] Likely a reference to Eduard Bernstein (1850-1932), a German Social Democrat and critic of Marxism.
[22] Mikhail Ivanovich Tugan-Baranovsky (1865-1919) was a Ukrainian economist and politician.

and for reasons that I shall mention, came a change. We had gotten over the top and in 1884 the panic was not quite so bad as in 1873 and in 1894 it was not so bad as it was in 1884, and in 1907 it was markedly less bad than in 1894 and today where we are again at the beginning of a period of depression and bad business and unemployment, we are no longer confronted by even the prospect of anything like that which happened in the 19th century. And what is still more true, we find that where socialism has been adopted as it has been adopted in Russia today, the lie again is given to the Marxian theory because the revolution has come not in a country where capitalism has been most developed but in the country where capitalism has been least developed.

Now, then, taking up the points in order, I want first to call attention to the achievements of capitalism. We are now not discussing what might have been attained under other conditions but simply what has been attained. What are the actual facts and the achievements of capitalism? I should sum them up as follows:

First and foremost, I should say that we must recognize the accumulation of wealth irrespective of where it is and in whose hands it is—the cheapening of production and the accumulation of wealth—because it is undeniable that certain advantages from this accumulation of capital and wealth accrue to the worker. Take as an example the railway system of this country with its twenty billions of capital, which would have been impossible in any preceding order of society and consider its benefits in taking the laborer to and from his work every day; take the accumulation of wealth as typified in this city in our public libraries, in our Natural Museum of History, in our Museum of Art and in all the other things which make for the convenience and pleasure of life. None of these things would have been possible, nor are they possible, nor have they ever been possible in a state of society where there has not been an accumulation of capital. [23] For while civilization indeed has its spiritual and indubitable ethical and religious ends, there is no doubt that civilization as we know it, even on the spiritual side, must needs be built up on a certain material basis and substructure. The accumulation of capital itself is an undoubted achievement.

In the second place, I should put the diversification of consumption. Compare the world today with what it was in all previous ages and consider what the laborer—even though he be the most poorly paid of all laborers—eats and what he wears and what he has with which to shelter himself. All of this is the result of the capitalist system. The bread which he eats comes from the wheat grown on the farms of North Dakota and milled in the great mills of Minneapolis and brought here by the railway. The meat which he consumes comes from the Far West of this country or perhaps from the pampas of Argentine. The tea which his family occasionally drinks

---

[23] The New York Public Library, in spite of its name, is a private institution, created via donations from wealthy industrialists like John Jacob Astor and Andrew Carnegie.

is brought from far off Cathay and the sugar with which he sweetens the cup comes from all parts of the world, from Cuba or the Far East. Even the tobacco with which he solaces his leisure hours may, for all he knows, come from Sumatra or from other portions of the Orient. And so it is with what he wears. His shoe is made of leather, tanned from the hides brought from the wilds of Siberia, the steppes of Russia or the plains of South America. The wool which makes his suit may come, for all he knows, from Australia and even the soap with which he occasionally washes himself— (laughter)—in all probability comes from the palm or the cocoa oil of Africa; while the trolley with which he goes to his work is built very largely of iron produced in the mills of Pittsburgh from the raw material from all parts of the West. This gigantic capitalist machine has rendered possible a diversification of consumption which has been unknown heretofore in the history of the world.

In the third place, capitalism is responsible for democracy. The democracy of classic antiquity was one based on sham, a pseudo-democracy resting upon slavery. The democracy even of our forefathers, when we declared our independence of England, was not a real democracy. It was an aristocracy. The policies of New Yorkers as late as 1800, at the time of Hamilton and Burr, were run by the great families precisely as in England. And it is false to claim as many have claimed that it is the frontier that has given us our democracy. We had a frontier in the 18th century, and we had no democracy. England has no frontier in the British Isles today and has produced a democracy. What has brought about democracy is the Industrial Revolution, or modern capitalism, and that means a public opinion which has never existed before in the history of the world. As a result, every workman, no matter how humble he be, today has democracy and enjoys a voice in influencing even to a small extent the management of the affairs of the state under which he lives.

In the fourth place, I should put as one of the achievements of capitalism, liberty of movement. In the Middle Ages, there was no liberty. The serf was bound to the soil and it is only since capitalism has developed that we have the modern liberty of movement, carrying with it as a result the liberty of production as well as the liberty of consumption.

And finally, to cap the climax, modern capitalism is responsible for education and for science. Never before in the history of the world have we had a form of public instruction comparable to our own. Weak though it be, defective though it be, sadly inadequate though it be, the amounts of money that are spent today in every modern capitalistic society for the public schools, for the education that goes down into the kindergarten and up into the state university, is something that the world before has never known. And science also is a direct product of capitalism. There was indeed a certain form of science among the Greeks, among the Arabs, etc. But science, by which we mean the unlocking of the secrets of nature, is distinctly a modern product. It began only with the introduction of modern capitalism and it is most strongly developed and progressive in the home of modern capitalism. And you all see why that is, because the modern businessman, in order to succeed must know the secrets of nature. He must secure the proof, and in order to get the proof he must employ and utilize those forms of organized investigation which we call science.

Now, ladies and gentlemen, those are great achievements. Never before in the several hundred-thousands or millions of years that man has been upon the Earth have such things been accomplished.

I do not deny indeed that there is a dark side as well, and to that I now come to address myself for a few minutes. What are the weaknesses and the excrescences[24] of capitalism? My point is that, since capitalism is a progressive form of society, these weaknesses are remediable, and these excrescences are being lopped off. What are those weaknesses? In the first place, we have unfair competition between businesses and human beings. But we all realize that this is gradually being done away with. A Jay Gould[25] or Jim Fiske[26] would be unthinkable in modern times; and even though in the railways we may still hear of the Rock Island or the Atchison or

---

[24] "A projection or outgrowth esp. when abnormal"—*Merriam-Webster's Collegiate Dictionary*, 11th Edition.

[25] Jason "Jay" Gould (1836-1902), American railroad magnate.

[26] James Fiske, Jr. (1835-1872), American stockbroker, associate of Jay Gould.

the New Haven and Hartford, we must remember that now for the first time in the history of our country, their forces are being harnessed up, and that the Interstate Commerce Commission[27] is now regulating the issue of securities which will render such things impossible in the future. What President Roosevelt did, among all his many accomplishments, was to so change certain forms of unfair competition as to make them more difficult. Society under modern capitalism, is gradually rendering competition more and more fair.

In the second place, we have, as one of these sad results, the fact that unjust privileges still continue and that certain forms of integrated organization known as "potential monopolies" sometimes make their appearance. But we find also that as soon as those evils are recognized they are being counteracted, and we have today in our Trade Commission and in many other forms of organization, a powerful counteragent which is gradually doing away with many forms of privilege.

In the third place, I should say that modern capitalism does result in exaggerated fortunes. The development of a leisure class has its bad sides at a time when everyone ought to be working. But what has society under modern capitalism done? A generation ago, I wrote a book on

---

[27] Created in 1887, the Interstate Commerce Commission was formed to regulate the railroads, to prevent "unjust discrimination between persons, places, commodities or particular descriptions of traffic."

progressive taxation[28] and I was attacked on all sides, by the reactionary and the stand-patter, on the ground that I was preaching confiscation. Nowadays, everyone, the capitalist like the others, not only believes in, but argues for progressive taxation. We have today gone further in this country than in any other—perhaps as some of us think even too far—with a system that takes up to 69.73% of a man's income, and in some cases even more. Progressive taxation is a sign of what modern capitalism is doing to restrict some of its own evils.

Now, when you come to the laborer there are of course very great evils, but they also are gradually being overcome. Take the conditions of work and the hours of work. Many years ago, the reform movement was for twelve hours a day. I remember the ten-hour-day movement. Then there came the great fight for the eight-hour day, and now some of our factory laws even permit only a six-hour day in certain industries. Capitalism itself is gradually changing those conditions. (Hearty laughter.) Capitalism is changing those conditions not because it likes to do it, but because it is compelled to do it by the letting loose of those very forces which are implicit in modern forms of capitalism. As it is with the hours, so with the wages. Wages are by no means what they ought to be. Wages are certainly far less than they should be. But wages have been growing during the last hundred

---

[28] *Progressive Taxation in Theory and Practice* (Baltimore: American Economic Association, 1894).

years, indubitably, and starting in Australia, going on to England, and now proceeding in this country, we have the great minimum-wage movement which is gradually improving those conditions.

And finally we come to the two great indictments of our present system: first, the insecurity of employment for the workman, that very great evil which is being attacked and which is entirely susceptible of being eradicated by the application of the same principle that we have applied to accidents, that we have applied to many other evils, namely, the insurance principle. There is no reason why the workman should be made to bear as he does today the burden of unemployment and of insecurity of tenure. (Applause.) We have already today in the unemployment insurance law of England the faint beginnings of a movement which I am convinced will spread within the next three or four decades like wildfire throughout the world. The regularization of industry must be brought about by industry itself with the aid of the state, and it is being brought about under modern methods.

And finally, the last point, the joylessness of life. That to a certain extent must continue under any form of industrial government, as long as we have the machine. Machines will be needed under socialism as under capitalism. But the real joylessness of the machine tender can be diminished, and can be partially done away with, by giving him more of a participation in the industry itself, as we are gradually doing through what we call "industrial democracy." By giving him more hours of leisure as we are gradually doing, we are giving him the time in which he can regain the joy which he loses in his work. The joylessness of industry is not so much the indictment of capitalism as it is the indictment of machinery. We must meet it and fight it and counter it wherever we can.

Now, ladies and gentlemen, in the few minutes that are left, I want to say a word to explain why, with all these reservations, I am not a socialist. (Laughter.) And I should put it in this way. In the first place, as regards the remuneration of labor, socialism preaches equal pay. A bonus, Lenin told us, was something only for bourgeois society. Equal pay means payment according to need. But, unfortunately, it is not payment according to need but rather according to efficient work that is really productive. Even in Russia today, they have been compelled (as you all know) to give up their original plans of payment according to need, and they now have developed the bonus system to a point even unheard of in the United States.

In the second place, let us deal with the other side of it, the man at the top. If society has progressed, at all events in some respects, it is due above all to the man who has been the leader, the leader in industry. Leaders are rare in industry. And while I am perfectly well aware of the new psychology which shows us the fallacy of the old economic man of Ricardo,[29] it remains none the less true that the real impulses and tendencies of human nature, the desire for distinction, for self-expression, for mastery, that all these things, after all, center themselves in the effort to do a little better than one's neighbor. We may not believe, as our great Emerson said, that we are all as lazy as we dare to be, but it is true that the race-horse does best when he has a pace-maker, and even we who sometimes play golf, don't play as well alone as when we play against a partner.

Now, ladies and gentlemen, under socialism, the possibilities of leadership would be restricted for two reasons: first, you would not have the incentive that you have now, and in the second place, the risk would be far more limited. Nowadays, people who get to the top through the selective process do so because they are willing and able to take risks. Under any form of socialistic government, the risk could not, would not be taken because they could not afford to take it. These two points, the selective process of the modern competitive system, and the restriction of the risk function in modern society, are to my mind the chief indictments against socialism.

Then we come finally to the restriction of liberty. I need only allude to certain socialists themselves who tell us what the other kinds of socialism would do in restraining

---

[29] David Ricardo (1772-1823), a leading British classical economist. "Economic man" is a model of human behavior, assumed by him (and many other economists) that man is rational and seeks to attain his desires with the least effort, i.e., he economizes.

liberty. But of that point we shall speak later. At all events you see why I am not a socialist. (Great and prolonged applause.)

Seligman portrait, from the published 1921 transcription.

Analysis of Affirmative

Seligman starts off with a crisp definition of capitalism—private ownership of the means of production—and then laments the various and diverse ways in which the term "socialism" is used, a plight with which the reader of our day can surely sympathize. He finally settles on a working definition, adopting the Marxist version, that under socialism, "the control of capital shall be in the hands of the group and that there shall be no room for private rent, private interest, or private profits." Nearing will later accept these definitions.

Seligman then asserts that, unlike socialism, there is only one form of capitalism, namely "progressive capitalism," which advances in time and geographically, and that it is still "in the very earliest stages of development."

I think this is a smart approach, and avoids the perennial asymmetry of such debates, where the socialist argues for the benefits of an ideal system, never yet experienced in its necessary perfection, while the capitalist is asked to defend the real-world present day, warts and all, or even worse, defend anything ever done in recorded history by anyone with money. Seligman tries to put capitalism on an equal footing, asserting that capitalism has perfections that it can approach as well, and has a history of actual improvements that can be pointed to.

Seligman then, quite effectively, lays out the accomplishments of capitalism. It has improved the condition of the poor as well as the rich. It has steadied the economy and reduced the occurrence of market panics and depressions. It has reduced unemployment. It has led to improved infrastructure like railroad lines, enjoyed by all. It has built up cultural institutions like museums, enjoyed by all. It has brought goods from around the country and around the world to our shops, for all to enjoy. It has brought an end to slavery and led to the emergence of a true democracy. It has enabled freedom of movement. It has improved science and education. "Now, ladies and gentlemen, those are great achievements. Never before in the several hundred-thousands or millions of years that man has been upon the Earth have such things been accomplished."

At the same time, not everything in the world is good. There is a dark side to capitalism as well. Seligman describes several: unfair competition, monopolies, excessive wealth, low wages, insecure employment, and the drudgery ("joylessness of life") of the factory worker tending a machine.

This is a good tactic. Seligman knows that his opponent will raise issues like these, and by mentioning them first and addressing them, he can frame the issues to his advantage.

Seligman then makes the critical point that merely debating the distribution of wealth in the world is insufficient. We also need to consider how it is that wealth comes about in the first place. Far from the claim of the socialists that the rich are getting richer while the poor are getting poorer, the experience with capitalism has been that all classes benefit. The worker under capitalism benefits directly, from his wages, but also indirectly from the increased prosperity of society as a whole.

Nearing portrait, from the 1921 published transcription.

Negative (Nearing)

Villard: Every American, whatever his economic beliefs, owes a debt of gratitude to the next speaker. He was one of those Americans who insisted, even in war time, upon that freedom of conscience and liberty to speak and write which are guaranteed by the Constitution of the United States.[30] (Great applause.) The foolish and blind law officers of a now utterly discredited administration sought to deprive him and us of the rights for which he stood and Mr. Scott Nearing went into the court and unlike some others placed in the same position, abated not one jot from the position which he had taken. (Great applause.) And with true intellectual heroism convinced a jury of American citizens that he was within his rights and this was still in some respects a free country. (Laughter.) I have the pleasure of presenting Scott Nearing. (Prolonged applause.)

---

[30] In April 1918 Nearing was indicted under the Espionage Act for alleged "obstruction to the recruiting and enlistment service of the United States." The basis for this was an anti-militaristic pamphlet Nearing authored, The Great Madness: A Victory for the American Plutocracy. In a jury trial in 1919 Nearing was acquitted. However, the publisher of the pamphlet, the American Socialist Society, was found guilty and fined $3,000.

Professor Seligman has given us what I consider two very satisfactory definitions of the issue before us this afternoon. He has defined capitalism as that form of industrial organization where the means of production, primarily the machines, are in the control of private individuals. He has defined socialism as the control of capital in the hands of the group, and under it there shall be no room for private rent, interest, or profit. Beginning as he does with these two definitions, I reach a somewhat dissimilar conclusion. (Laughter.) I do not see capitalism in so rosy a light as does Professor Seligman and I want to try to explain to you in the brief time that I have why not, and what the socialists propose to put in its place, and I want to explain them under three headings: first, the ownership of the machinery of production, second, the control arising out of such ownership, third the direction resulting from such control. And I want to try to demonstrate to you that under capitalism the worker has to accept, first, intermittent starvation, second, slavery, and third, war. (Applause.)

Professor Seligman says that capitalism is progressive. So are some diseases. (Hearty laughter and applause.) Under the present system of society, a little group of people own resources, machines, capital, all of the machinery upon which forty million workers depend for their living. That is, the capitalist owns the job. The capitalist owns the job without which the worker dies of starvation. The worker therefore must go to the capitalist and ask for permission to work. To what extent has this ownership been concentrated in the United States? I wish that I could answer that intelligently, but the best that I can do is to cite you the 1918 income tax returns. In that year, 1918, you remember that prices were about what they are now. In that year, $200 a week was not a fortune by any means. $200 a week was not much wealth in 1918.[31] But there were only 160,000 people in this whole United States who reported incomes of as much as $200 a week. That is, fourteen persons in every thousand of the population, four persons for every thousand gainfully employed, one family for every five hundred families in the land, with incomes of $10,000 a year, $200 a week. They tell us that Rome and Assyria and Babylon and those old countries reached a point of concentration where 1% of the people owned the wealth of the empires. I say to you in America, 1918, four in every thousand of those gainfully employed earned $200 a week.

I wish I could give you the figures of ownership but I could not collect them. Senator Pettigrew in 1890 had the census take an estimate of wealth and since 1890 every census has specifically excluded any estimate of wealth

---

[31] Inflation-adjusted, $200.00/week in April 1918 is $3,667.44/week in October 2020, or $190,706.88/year. See: https://www.bls.gov/data/inflation_calculator.htm

ownership in the United States.[32] Be that as it may, I need not stress the point. The facts speak for themselves. We have in America a little handful of people owning the railroads, the banks, manufactories, mining, and other establishments and to them go tens of millions of men and women asking for jobs, for the right to make a living. But the master, the owner replies, "In order to have a job, you must produce—produce something for yourself and something for me and the interest, dividends, profits, returns, for which I do not labor." Said Abraham Lincoln in 1858: "A slave society is one in which one class says to another class, you work and toil and earn bread and we will eat it."[33] These owners of American capital, these

---

[32] Richard F. Pettigrew (1848-1926), Senator for North Dakota. Like Nearing, Pettigrew was charged under the Espionage Act for his anti-war statements, charges that were later dropped. In his analysis of the 1890 census, Pettigrew observed that, "52 percent of the people, or two percent more than half of them, owned but five per cent of the accumulated wealth of the United States" in R.F. Pettigrew, Imperial Washington (Chicago C.H. Kerr, 1922), 121.

[33] The actual quote, from the 7th Lincoln-Douglas debate (Oct. 15, 1858) was: "It is the eternal struggle between these two principles—right and wrong—throughout the world. They are the two principles that have stood face to face from the beginning of time; and will ever continue to struggle. The one is the common right of humanity, and the other the divine right of kings. It is the same principle in whatever shape it develops itself. It is the same spirit that says, 'You toil and work and earn bread, and I'll eat it.' No matter in what shape it comes, whether from the mouth of a king who seeks to bestride the people of his own nation and live by the fruit of their labor, or from one race of men as an apology for enslaving another race, it is the same tyrannical principle."

stock and bond holders say to the American worker, "You work and toil and earn bread and we will eat it."

How much do they get of the bread produced by the workers? Get a copy of Senate Document 259.[34] You can't get a copy because they were not distributed. Get a copy of that document of profiteering and find out how much they made in 1917—hundreds, thousands of percent of profit in a single year—in America, the richest of rich countries! In America, the center of the greatest empire on Earth, we report 26% of our school children underfed in the schools. We reported that before the present economic unpleasantness began. (Applause and laughter.) We reported that while we were still urging the worker to produce and while he was turning out not only enough for his own daily sustenance, but in addition enough to provide the capitalist with a surplus and that surplus went to the front and we burned it in Europe and then the war was over and we burned a bit of it here at home and the burning got too expensive. The worker received less in wages than he had created in product. He could not buy back the volume that he had produced.

---

[34] The report was apparently entitled, "Corporate Earnings and Government Revenue." I have not been able been able to locate a copy, although it was a common topic of speculation in newspapers at the time. From that coverage it sounds like the report looked at earnings per invested capital, for companies where this value exceeded 15%. Critiques at the time noted that this calculation failed to account for the contribution of retained earnings (profits reinvested in the business) accumulated over years.

The capitalist, the owner of the shop did not need to use what had been produced and given to him as surplus. He wanted to dispose of it. The war gave him a chance. Exports gave him some chance but then that chance was ended and the capitalist said to the worker last April, last May, last June, the capitalist said to the worker, "There will be no more work." And in textiles, boots, and shoes, automobiles and now later in steel and other industries, they are laying them off. I got a report from the New York State Industrial Commission this week: 643,000 men and women out of work in New York State. What have they done? Why, they cannot have work. But what have they done? Why, they have produced too much. They have created too great a surplus. They must wait to produce more until this surplus is consumed. Can they consume it? No! Because they did not receive enough wages to buy it back. (Applause.) And so, in this country today, three million people are out of work. You do not see these figures stated in the newspapers.

In the first six months of 1920, the average number of commercial failures per month was 500; in July, 598; August, 633; September, 661; October, 802; November, 892; December, 1,854; the first three weeks of January, 1,482; and so the number mounts. Professor Seligman has already referred to this. I have a book here called A History of Panics in the United States written by a

Frenchman, translated by an American business man,[35] and this book gives a record of the panics that we have had under capitalism: "1814, 1818, 1826, 1837, 1848, 1857, 1864, 1873, 1884, 1893, 1897, 1903, 1907, 1913"—and 1921. (Laughter).

That book contains one of the most damning indictments that has ever been written on capitalism. "Capitalism," says the author, "consists of three phases: prosperity, panic, and liquidation." (Laughter.) Prosperity is the period when the dinner pail is full and the hopes are high, when the little man drops his tools and leaves his bench, borrows his capital, buys a machine and goes into business. Panic is the period when the little fellows get the tools and the machines shaken out of their hands and start back for the bench, and liquidation is the period when the big fellows pick up what is around loose, put it in their pockets and go off richer than they were before. (Hearty laughter and applause.)

"Progressive," says Seligman. I say "No! Successive." And as long as capitalism lasts, so long will men and women, by the millions, walk the streets looking for work and so long will their gas bills be paid and their children starve—successive starvation, successive periods of physical misery and death from lack of physical means

---

[35] Presumably, a reference to: Clement Juglar and DeCourcy W. Thom (trans.), *A Brief History of Panics and their Periodical Occurrence in the United States,* 3rd Edition (New York: G.P. Putnam's Sons, 1916).

in the center of the greatest wealth that the world knows. That is what capitalism has to offer the world. (Applause.)

What do we Socialists want? Why, we want to own these things ourselves. (Laughter.) As we own the Harbor of New York, so we want to own the coal mines, the railroads, the factories, in order that no surplus may be produced, in order that the value of product shall be represented by the value paid to a consumer. (Applause.) So that he who creates can buy back the value that he creates. (Applause.) Quite simple and quite inevitable in the long run.

But I don't stress that point. It is not essential. It is my second point about which I wish to talk—about slavery. "Whenever a man says to another man, 'You go and work and earn bread and I will eat it,' said Lincoln, "it is slavery." That is capitalism and that is my chief charge against capitalism and that is the thing that we socialists set up as our highest hope in socialism, not that it will give us more bread, but that it will give us steadier bread, more regular bread, more bread, and not that we will get more to eat out of socialism but that we will get more liberty. That is where we place our hope and I want to explain the contrast because it is fundamental.

The United States I said was owned by capitalists—worse than that owned by capitalist corporations—owned impersonally, not by individuals who have made their pile and bought their machinery, owned by trusts, owned by great organizations with their stocks and their bonds and their big business mechanisms. I wish I had time to read you this last report of the National City Bank to show you how that ownership works out. Here is a list of the board of directors. This is the biggest bank in North America. Here is a list of board of directors: Percy A. Rockefeller, William Rockefeller, J. Ogden Armour, Nicholas F. Brady of the New York Edison Company, Cleveland H. Dodge, Philip A. S. Franklin, etc.

What is the National City Bank? Why, it is the center of a great web of economic power. Here is the report issued by the Pujo Committee.[36] At the center of the spider's web, they put a great banking concern, J. P. Morgan & Company and around that banking concern, they group railroads, public utilities, industries, mines, and other forms of industrial enterprise. At the center of the power lies the strength and the weakness of the system, lies the banker. I have not time to dwell on that further than to call your attention to this fact that the Federal Reserve System with its 30,000 banks and its board of directors, sitting in one place around the table, has more power than any single institution on the face of the civilized Earth, and that Federal Reserve System is in private hands. It is privately owned, practically. It is under government supervision, yes, but the Federal Reserve System is the nerve center, the center of authority, the center of power,

---

[36] A House subcommittee that investigated J.P. Morgan and his associates in 1912-13.

and what are they going to do with this control that they exercise through their banking machine?

I want to read you a paragraph from a weekly letter sent by one business house to its clients. "The war taught employing classes in America the secret and power of widespread propaganda. Now, when we have anything to sell to the American people, we know how to sell it. We have learned. We have the schools; we have the pulpit." The employing class owns the press, the economic power centering in the banks, schools, pulpit, press, movie screen, all the power of widespread propaganda now. "When we have something to sell to the American people, we know how to sell it." Slavery: going to the boss and asking for the privilege of a job. Slavery: sending your child to school and having him pumped full of virulent propaganda in favor of the present system. (Great applause.) Slavery in every phase of life all tied up under this one banker's control.

Is it true that no man is good enough to rule another man without that man's consent? Is that still true in America or in the world? If that be true, every worker in the shop shall have the right to say who shall exercise authority over him in the shop. Every worker in an industry has the right to pick these or help these members as board of directors. Do you suppose the workers in the National City Bank elected William Rockefeller and Percy Rockefeller and J. Ogden Armour? (Laughter.)

In the United States, a worker goes to work on a machine owned by the boss. He works on materials owned by the boss. He turns out a product owned by the boss. He lives in a country where the organized power of the boss concentrated in the banking system is supreme over every phase of life. He is a slave—industrial slave—because he cannot call one economic right his own and we socialists want to have industry not only owned by those who participate in it but we want to have those who participate in industry direct the industry in which they participate. Industrial self-control, self-government in industry as Mr. Cole[37] has put it—that is all—simple ideas, ownership by the worker of his own job, the control by a man of his own economic life.

And third, I spoke about the direction of industry. I read you the report of the last annual meeting of the United States Steel Corporation. At this meeting, according to the New York Times, here was voted two million and one-quarter shares of common, and one and one-half million shares of preferred stock. Stockholders who attended the meeting represented 340 shares of preferred and 4,000 shares of common and the rest were voted by proxy—so many million shares on this side, so many million shares on this side, and the policy of the United States Steel Corporation is formed and unionism is crushed out and this or that line of industrial policy is pursued by a little

---

[37] G.D.H. Cole (1889-1959), professor at Oxford, guild socialist, author of *Self-Government in Industry* (1917).

handful of men and women who have nothing better to do with their leisure time than to go and sit through a meeting of the United States Steel Corporation stockholders. That is the biggest corporation in America, direction not only by absentee ownership but direction by little cliques of lawyers holding proxies in their hands, by executives of great industries speaking in the name of stockholders.

And what did they do? Last year, in the United States, that is in 1919, they floated twelve thousand-millions of new capital stock and bonds; 1920 they floated fourteen thousand-millions of new capital stocks and bonds. Did you have any say in that? Does the worker speak when it is decided to put these twenty-five billions into new capital under circumstances when it is almost certain that it cannot function? Did the workers speak? No, it was done by voting shares. They go out into Thrace. They support General Wrangel.[38] They go down into Mexico. They follow into Hayti. And then what happens? Other stockholders in other countries, Royal Dutch Shell stockholders, British stockholders, voting policy against Standard Oil; Standard Oil stockholders, if they ever vote, voting policy against Royal Dutch Shell; and you hear the echoes of the conflict over the markets of France and you hear the echoes of their conflict for the rights in Central Europe. What is going to be the result? When will it be

---

[38] General Baron Pyotr Nikolayevich Vrangel (1878-1928), commander of the White Army forces who opposed the Bolshevik Red Army during the Russian Civil War. After the war he lived in exile in Brussels.

necessary to put the war paint on the battleships? When will it be necessary again to call out the battalions and send them? In 1914 Great Britain had a highway to the sea. Germany wanted it. A pistol shot sounds in Central Europe and ten million men go to their graves to decide that Great Britain shall hold Baghdad and that Germany shall pay what she can. (Applause.)

In 1914, there was not a socialist state in Europe—capitalist Germany, capitalist France, capitalist Russia, capitalist Italy, capitalist Britain—all the great group of capitalist empires grabbing the world to rob it, and fighting one another to the death to determine who should have the right to do the plundering. They produced a surplus, as I said. They could not spend it at home. They took it abroad, and in the course of taking it abroad they had to make war—capitalist war—and working men went and fought and died in that capitalistic war which they told us, through their propaganda machinery, was a war for democracy. (Applause.) What does the worker want? Why, he wants to keep the strings of economic life himself. Capitalism offers him intermittent starvation, industrial slavery, recurring war. Socialism offers him subsistence, economic self-government, a basis for peace.

And I would like to ask Professor Seligman, if he and I were miners up in Panther Creek, in the Philadelphia Reading Coal and Iron Company, whether he would be an ardent supporter of the present economic system. (Great applause.) And I want to ask him this further question, whether under those circumstances, he would put any obstacle in the way of the coming of some such system as I have described to you. (Great and prolonged applause.)

Analysis of Negative

Nearing follows with a well-honed argument. At its core it is straight-from-the-book Marxism-Leninism but Nearing clothes it in a folksy popular appeal. It is worth a closer look to see how Nearing puts the argument together.

Capitalism is based on a form of slavery, that the capitalist employer "owns the job" and can effectively starve the worker. This is also seen in the fact that the capitalists (who do not labor) earn a profit, which means that the workers, as a whole, cannot afford to buy the product of their labors.

This is followed by a recitation of various economic statistics to illustrate economic inequality, suggesting there is even more data to support this, data which is secret or hidden, with insinuations of a government conspiracy to keep such data from the public, e.g., that since 1890 the federal census was no longer tracking personal wealth, that a U.S. Senate report on war profiteering was being withheld from the public, that the newspapers were hiding the real unemployment numbers, etc.

Not only do the capitalists effectively expropriate their profits from the workers under threat of starvation, but the capitalists have no way of consuming this profit domestically. They are forced to seek out investment opportunities in less developed nations, in South America, in the Middle East, in Asia, and in Africa. It is the rush of capital into these nations which brought the great powers into conflict and led to Word War I.

Nearing then notes that, with the Great War now over, demand for matériel, here and abroad, has come down, and the resulting surplus in capacity has depressed some industries, leading to unemployment. He then makes the most curious argument that the real problem here is the workers are not being paid enough. If only the workers were paid the "full value" of their labor, they would be able to afford their own products, and the surplus would disappear. Among other flaws in this argument, it assumes that the mix of goods desired in peacetime is identical to those desired in wartime.

Most of this is standard Marxist fare. If you accept the now-discredited Labor Theory of Value then the profit of the capitalist represents the exploitation of the worker. A Marxist need not even slow down to argue this point. It follows from their definitions.

Added to this narrative is the argument, taken from Lenin's 1917 pamphlet "Imperialism: The Highest Stage of Capitalism," to explain how capitalist nations have (temporarily) delayed the ultimate exploitation of their workers by instead exploiting poorer nations. This should be a familiar rhetorical technique. Many ecos-ocialists argue today that the reason why capitalism has not collapsed yet is that we (temporarily) are now exploiting the environment.

Finally, after indicating a problem to be solved (economic inequality, market panics, war) and suggesting the ultimate causes of these ills (capitalism, capitalism, capitalism), Nearing now offers his solution: worker ownership of the job and of the machinery, worker control of the enterprise, industrial self-government, "the control by a man of his own economic life."

Affirmative Rebuttal (Seligman)

Villard: Professor Seligman now has 20 minutes for rebuttal. (Great applause.)

If I were the coal miner in Pennsylvania (I think that was the miner that was mentioned), I should say that the answer had already been given by Mr. Nearing. (Laughter.) Mr. Nearing said that he wanted socialism in order that no surplus shall be produced. That is my objection to socialism. (Applause.) The world has progressed in civilization only because every generation did not consume all that it produced, but that it laid by a surplus. (Applause.) Under socialism, ladies and gentlemen, not alone will no surplus be laid by, but from my point of view, the conditions of production will be so far inferior that even the amount available for consumption on the part of the laborer will be less than it is today. If I were therefore an intelligent coal miner, I would say I should rather live in the coal mines of Pennsylvania with a chance (at all events, once in a while) of getting something to eat rather than to live under a condition, let us say, like that of China today, where, without capitalism, starvation is not alone intermittent but almost continuous. (Laughter.)

Now, the second point. We have heard the old story retold to us that life is impossible for the working man because the capitalist owns the job and does not need the working man. How long would the shareholders of the United States Steel Corporation, if that were all they had to live on, how long would they continue to enjoy their luxuries if the workmen all stopped work permanently? (Applause.) Does the workman need the job giver any more than the job giver needs the workman? And my point is, where you have those conditions under which leadership can develop to create new jobs, the workman will be far better off than where he has control alone of his own lob. (Slight applause.) Don't mistake me. One point in which Mr. Nearing did not meet me at all, but which I trust he will meet in his rebuttal is this: that while we may be entirely favorable to the aspirations and the hopes and the desires of the great mass of the working population, he must prove that forces are not at work under capitalism which will meet and realize those hopes and those aspirations.

Now, Mr. Nearing says, "I put my chief argument on the score of liberty." Let us see what we can make of that. We have at the present time a form of socialism in operation, the only realization of a practical socialism on a large scale with which the world has ever been confronted. How does the workman fare there with liberty? By chance, I happen to have in my possession a reprint of some of the official documents and statements issued during the last few months in Russia and I shall take up part of my time by reading how it stands with liberty under socialism. First, I have the resolution of the Petrograd government printing office workers of two months ago. "Our workday lasts twelve hours. We are compelled to work in two shifts in the paper department of our factory and we have to work both Saturdays and Sundays. No exception is made with regard to women; since August 15th, overtime work has become compulsory." There you have liberty. (Laughter and applause.)

In the second place, I have extracts from The Metallurgist, an organ of the metallurgical workers. "At our factory, absolute submission to the administration of the plant has been established. No arguments or interference with its orders on the part of the workers are tolerated. At our factory, failure to report for work without permission is punishable by forfeiture of extra food. The same punishment is meted out for refusal to do compulsory overtime work. For being late on the job, two days food are deducted."

And here comes the resolution of all the Petrograd workers on September 5th, as a result of the liberty of socialism: "We feel as if we were hard labor convicts where everything has been subject to iron rules. We have become lost as human beings and have been turned into slaves." There is your socialistic liberty. (Great applause.)

And how does socialism deal with the strike? Let me read you the report of the decision of the commissar of the special commission at the railway works. "All active strikers shall be turned over to the Extraordinary Commission for the purpose of sending them to forced labor." And what does the commission do? Here is the report. "The strike at our works ended, thanks to numerous arrests among the strikers. Concerning the fate of twelve of our workers, we have no news. The Extraordinary Commission refuses all information about them. As far as we can learn they have been shot." There is liberty under socialism.

And finally, the last extract that I shall read to you is the report of the President of the Petrograd Commune to a delegation from the workers of a certain city who complained of being starved and not getting enough to eat. "Yes, we do admit," he says, "that the food allowance is insufficient, but at the same time we also know full well—this has been taught by real life—that as long as the worker or plain citizen is busy obtaining food he takes no interest in politics. Just give the workingman enough to eat today and you will hear him cry tomorrow for civic liberties." "Our object," says the socialistic government, "is to keep the workers just from dying; and that is what we are doing." (Applause.)

What is the use of prating about these beautiful ideals, the fabric of the imagination? As soon as you get socialism into practice—and mind you, Messrs. Lenin and Trotsky would be very wroth if you accused them of being anything else but socialists—as soon as you get socialism into practice, you get the very same results that you will get whenever a body of determined, and intolerant men attempt to realize their misguided ideal.

Now then, I think I have disposed of liberty under socialism, to my satisfaction at least—(laughter)—mind you, furthermore, what I have read is borne out by the socialist writers themselves. Take Mr. Cole who has just been mentioned; To quote from one of his works, he says that "State socialism is a bureaucratic and Prussianizing movement." His substitute is the milk-and-water guild socialism which has made little progress even among our parlor socialists in this country. It scarcely deserves a refutation because it is bound to be so inefficient, bound as even its latest advocates tell us, to result in all sorts of competition between the guilds and bound to result in this very absurd state of affairs where you will have an industrial parliament and state and then some super-monstrosity on top of it. It scarcely deserves the discussion of intelligent people The real socialism with which we have to cope is the socialism of which Mr. Nearing speaks, the socialism of Lenin, the socialism of Trotsky, the socialism of those who start out with beautiful ideals and who are compelled by the grim facts of everyday life to seek to do away with starvation through tyranny.

Now, ladies and gentlemen, another point to which Mr. Nearing did not reply, is the progressive character, not of the disease but of the remuneration to the workers. Mr. Nearing himself is responsible for a book on wages and from the same statistics which he utilizes, another writer, Professor King, has constructed a book which sums up the matter very much better perhaps than in almost any other production. (Laughter.)

In 1850 the average wages were $204. In 1910, the average wage—mind you, the average wage of the average workman, taking the low and high altogether, had gone up to $507. Allowing for the difference in the purchasing power of money, wages had risen from 1850, $147 up to 1910, $401. Now, gentlemen, I ask Mr. Nearing whether he denies these facts, and if not, how he explains that there is not a progressive tendency in capitalism. (Laughter.)

Now, let us come to another point that he makes. He said that a great deal is gotten by individuals for which they do not labor. All that is produced by the worker, practically all is filched from him by the recipient of profits and interest. Now, ladies and gentlemen, I think many of you know of some of the things that have been accomplished in this country. When Mr. James J. Hill,[39] the great "Empire Builder," built one of the transcontinental railroads which have brought about the cheapening of products and the diversification of consumption of which I spoke, did he not contribute to production? When Mr. McCormick[40] invented and finally utilized the reaper and the thresher and the mower, which have revolutionized the work of the farmer and the whole life of the community and built up a fortune, did he not contribute to

---

[39] James J. Hill (1838-1916), CEO of the Great Northern Railway, produced a transcontinental line without public funds.
[40] Cyrus McCormick (1809-1884), American inventor, founder of McCormick Harvesting Machine Company.

production? When Mr. Westinghouse[41] invented the air brake and finally reaped a fortune by utilizing it in the uttermost parts of the world, did he not contribute to production? And when our friend Mr. Ford with whose general philosophy perhaps I am not in entire accord— (laughter)—when he brought down the price of automobiles, the automobiles that are used by the workmen all over this country in going to and from their daily work. (Hearty laughter.) I passed by a factory the other day and found that there were 550 automobiles. They did not happen to be all Ford automobiles. And I stepped in and said, "To whom do they belong?" And I was told, "Each one of these belongs to a workman in this factory. They come every morning and go back every evening." Now then, could those fortunate workmen say that Mr. Ford has been able to heap up his millions by simply taking them, filching them, stealing them, from the men in his employ?

Ladies and gentlemen, there we come to the real inwardness of the whole situation. I do not deny that there is theft. I do not deny that there is robbery. I do not deny that there are bad people as well as good people, but I do say that the essence of the capitalist system today, that the essence of profits today, of legitimate profits, is not theft but service, and that people in the long run cannot under modern conditions, in the long run and under

---

[41] George Westinghouse (1846-1914), American engineer. He also was an active promoter of alternating current, directly opposing Edison's direct current system in what was called the "War of Currents."

normal conditions, make great profits unless they really do service for the community. The distinction that is sought to be made by the socialist, that the private capitalist is a thief and that the socialist community alone gives service, flies in the face of all the progress that has been made during the last few decades.

And finally, we come to Mr. Nearing's reference to war. I do not deny that war has been due to all manner of causes. We have had dynastic wars. We have had personal wars. We have had religious wars. We have had trade wars. We have had capitalistic wars. But that is no reason for ascribing all wars to capitalism or for saying that if we were to have socialism, war would come to an end. And moreover, so far as capitalism is concerned, mark again these progressive symptoms and manifestations. We are a capitalistic nation. What have we done with Cuba? What have we done with the Philippines?[42] (Laughter.) What we have done is to educate them, to develop their economic resources, to put them in the position where they are almost ready, and will soon be entirely ready, for self-government. (Laughter.) I maintain that a capitalistic community which is able to say that it can deal with its colonies, in the spirit of what I call progressiveness, that such a community is not entirely destitute of hope.

---

[42] A reference to American intervention in the Cuban War of Independence (1895) and the Philippine Revolution (1896).

And now finally, I want to ask Mr. Nearing two questions: first, if he is a socialist, does he believe in Lenin and Trotsky—(laughter)—and second, if he believes in Lenin and Trotsky does he think that the kind of liberty that is given under that socialism is symptomatic of socialism in general? (Prolonged applause.)

Analysis of Affirmative Rebuttal

Seligman takes on the accusation that the presence of surpluses is an evil and destabilizing aspect of capitalism. He argues that creating surpluses is a prime source of progress and prosperity. Although he does not use the term here, he could have argued that surplus is the source of all investment as well.

A more subtle observation here is that Seligman is equivocating on the term "surplus," and that Nearing did as well. They seem to be using the term for three different things: 1) Surplus as the unearned value received by the capitalist in excess of the amount paid to the workers, i.e., the profit, 2) Surplus as the production of a factory in excess of current demand, i.e., goods piling up in inventory, unsold, and 3) Surplus as income exceeding current consumption needs, which is saved. Seligman and Nearing were smart fellows. They knew what they were doing. This equivocation was for rhetorical purposes, to stun and dazzle the audience.

Seligman then counters the claim that the factory owner "owns the job" by pointing out that employment is a mutually-beneficial relationship, that the wealthy industrialist would quickly be in a sad place if he had no workers. "Does the workman need the job giver any more than the job giver needs the workman?"

Seligman then introduces a variety of first-hand reports on the conditions in Russia, of how the workingmen are doing, showing that their workdays are longer, conditions more brutal, that they have no say in how the workplace is run, that strikes are illegal and harshly punished, that they are being intentionally starved so that they have no energy for complaining, and that they feel that they are essentially slaves.

Again, to avoid the unfair comparison of real-world capitalism with imaginary or ideal socialism, Seligman must bring to light the reality on the ground. He came well-prepared to address each of Nearing's claims.

Seligman then argues that the industrialist has earned his profit by the inventions and efficiencies he has brought into being, which have led to increased prosperity for all. "[T]he essence of the capitalist system today, that the essence of profits today, of legitimate profits, is not theft but service, and that people in the long run cannot under modern conditions, in the long run and under normal conditions, make great profits unless they really do service for the community."

He wraps up with a short dismissal of Nearing's claims regarding capitalist wars, noting that wars have many causes, and that, far from being rapacious, the United States has been a liberator, in Cuba and in the Philippines.

Negative Rebuttal (Nearing)

Villard: Mr. Nearing has twenty minutes for rebuttal (Applause).

∼

"Is there any," says Professor Seligman, "progressive tendency in capitalism?" Yes, I think so. I think he has a little overdone it in assuming all of the virtues of the Industrial Revolution as the sole right and sole property of capitalism. All of the advantages of the machine will not accrue solely to capitalism. He told you that wages had risen since 1840 (I think), production has increased, locomotives have been brought in, incandescent lights have been put up—all of these things during the capitalist era. Would they have been done if there had been no capitalism? I cannot answer that. But I want to assure you that these same railroads and these same incandescent lights will be installed all over Europe, all over Asia and Africa, before we get through with it, whether under capitalism or under socialism. The product of the machine is a heritage of the race now, and not a peculiar product of capitalism, nor can it be claimed today by any particular social scheme.

Do I regard capitalism as progressive? Yes. We have had progressive panics—I call them successive panics—ever since 1814, and I defy Professor Seligman to show that under the capitalist method of one man owning the job, another man working it, and the job owner getting a part of the product of the worker in the form of a surplus—I defy Professor Seligman to show you under those circumstances there will not be successive panics. That is, under capitalism intermittent starvation will be the lot of the worker and tinkering with the capitalist system will not stop it. (Applause.)

Under capitalism industrial slavery is progressive. In the early days of capitalism any man could get a job by going out to the frontier and taking a farm. The frontier is gone. Capital is required in large quantities. If you want to open a successful business, it needs tens or hundreds of thousands of dollars. Only a few can start in business. Most of us must remain workers. The old factory was a little two-by-four concern. The modern factory employs you with a thousand or five thousand others. It locks you in a great city. It shoots you back and forth, not in Ford cars, but in subways, elevators, and other similar means of transportation. (Laughter and applause.) You have become a part of a mechanism that is growing continually harder, more set, more firmly established, where the chance to rise out of the ranks of the workers is diminishing. That is progressive also. There is no doubt that capitalism is progressive, and, as I said at the beginning, that industrial slavery is progressing faster than anything else. Among other things, thirty-five states have now established peacetime espionage acts.[43]

Then there is another thing that is progressive under capitalism. I refer to war. I have a little article here called "An Economic Interpretation of the War," written by Professor Seligman.[44] (Laughter.) He found an author on "Wages" that did better than I did, but I have not found anybody on the war that has been better than Professor Seligman. (Hearty laughter and applause.) So, I am going to quote what he has to say. (Laughter.)

> While economic considerations indeed do not by any means explain all national rivalry, they often illumine the dark recesses of history and afford on the whole the most weighty and satisfactory interpretation of modern national contests which are not clearly referable to purely racial antagonisms alone.

And then he goes ahead to develop the idea of the struggle for trade, the idea of the struggle for markets, progressing up through the various stages of modern industrial society.

---

[43] Probably a reference to "criminal syndicalism" laws which most states passed during the Red Scare of 1917-1920. Such laws provided for hightened penalties for the commission of a crime for political or industrial reform purposes.

[44] A pamphlet published in 1915, a reprint of Seligman's chapter in the multi-author compilation, Problems of Readjustment After the War.

> The most important phase of modern industrial capitalism still remains to be explained. After national industry has been built up through a period of protection, and after the developed industrial countries have replaced the export of raw material by the export of manufactured commodities, there comes a time when the accumulation of industrial and commercial profits is such that a more lucrative use of the surplus can be made abroad in the less developed countries than at home with the lower rates usually found in an older industrial system. In other words, the emphasis is now transferred from the export of goods to the export of capital.

That, says Professor Seligman, was the stage of Britain before this war. Germany had just reached that stage. With what result?

> To say, then, that either Great Britain or Germany is responsible for the present war, seems to involve a curiously short-sighted view of the situation. Both countries, nay, all the countries of the world, are subject to the sweep of these mighty forces over which they have but slight control, and by which they are one and all pushed on with an inevitable fatality.

The war is over. Germany is gone. But Japan and Great Britain, and the United States each have tens of billions of surplus accumulation capital that must be exported, and those great forces that swept Europe into the catastrophe of 1914, as Professor Seligman says, are now sweeping Japan, Great Britain and the United States into even a greater disaster, those same progressive forces of capitalism. (Applause.) Yes, it is progressive. It goes right on building up intermittent starvation, industrial slavery, war. They are in the system and they are part of it.

There is also a progressive tendency in socialism. I spent last summer in Europe. It is like going from—well, shall I say it is like going in summertime from a hot basement room into a refrigerating plant. You get a breath that makes you stand up and feel almost at home again. All over Europe is growing the spirit of solidarity among the workers. Why, last summer when they tried to make a war between Russia on the one hand, and England and France on the other,[45] the workers of France organized— ex-soldiers, socialists, labor unionists, all got together with the slogan, "Not a man, not a *sou*,[46] not a shell for imperial Poland against working-class Russia." (Great

---

[45] Since the Russian Revolution occurred before World War I ended, the Allied powers had the primary objective of reducing the benefit Germany and the Axis powers would receive from Russia's withdrawal. A small number of Allied troops occupied strategic points in Russia to secure war supplies, rail lines, oil fields, etc., and prevent them from falling into German hands.

[46] A French five-centime copper coin.

applause.) In Great Britain seven million men appointed a Council of Action, and they said to the British Cabinet, "If you inaugurate a war with Soviet Russia, within twenty-four hours every wheel of every basic industry on the British Isles will stop turning." (Applause) … solidarity growing all over Europe. The miners met, the transportation workers met, the metal workers met, the railway workers met during this crisis last August, and one and all passed resolutions declaring that if they tried to make a war on Russia they would not transport, they would not manufacture, they would not ship, they would not handle war products of any kind—solidarity growing, the sense of solidarity everywhere.

Even here in the United States it is growing. It cannot show its head now and then, but it is growing everywhere among the working people. (Applause.) The Russian Revolution came in 1917, came almost out of a clear sky, came because the old system in Russia had broken down under three years of war, and the Russian workers, ill-prepared, without technical experience, lacking transportation, unequipped with machinery, the Russian workers undertook to set up a new social order.

The old order had been the order of the czar. The new order was based on this section of their constitution— "He that will not work, neither shall he eat"—a phrase that runs back at least two thousand years. That is the idea they set out on, that the workers should be the basis of this new order of society. In the Russia of the czars the basis of power had been the loafers, the professional aristocrats. In the new society, said the Constitution of the Soviets, "He that will not work, neither shall he eat nor vote." That was the new order they tried to set up. Well, what happened? They made a "sanitary cordon" about Russia. They inaugurated a blockade. Japan, France, and the United States sent in their armies and they made war on Russia. We sent in our army to save the Russian people from the Bolsheviki. (Laughter.) Our soldiers were not cordially received. Neither were the other allied troops. That fell down, and it fell down because the soldiers of allied Europe would not go there to fight.

And then we tried another stunt. There was Yudenich, there was Deniken, there was Kolchak,[47] and there were all these other adventurers making civil war. And we gave them money, supplies, munitions, furnished them with equipment, and said, "Go to it, boys. Stir up as much trouble as you can." And that did not work. They have just gotten rid of Mr. Wrangel over in Russia. And then we financed all the little countries. Why, last summer French officers were directing the Polish army, and the New York Times published a picture of a brigade of Polish soldiers equipped with American, British, and French uniforms and equipment. For three years we denied them medicine. For three years we denied them food. For three years we starved their women and children while we

---

[47] General Nikolai Yudenich (1862-1933), Lieutenant General Anton Denikin (1872-1947), and Admiral Alexander Kolchak (1874-1920) were Imperial Army and Navy officers who led White forces in the Russian Civil War.

supported insurrection at home and made war on them abroad—for three years after they had already had three years of war! And now Professor Seligman wants to know whether that is a fair example of what socialism can do. (Thunderous and prolonged applause.)

Professor Seligman wants to know what I think of Lenin and Trotsky. Now I will tell him if I can—(laughter)—and in a word. I think that when the history of this period comes to be written that there is not a man nor a woman in this hall this afternoon whose name will stand that high (indicating) with the names of Lenin and Trotsky in this period. (Great applause.) There are not two braver men in the world today, men who have stood up in the face of great opposition and steadily have worked for the end in which they believe. Do I agree with their theories? With some of them I agree, and with some of them I don't. You could not agree with both Lenin and Trotsky because they don't agree with one another. (Laughter and applause.) But just as I regard the Russian Revolution as the greatest event in history since 1676,[48] just as I regard it as the epoch-making event, the dividing line between capitalism and socialism, so I regard these two men as two of those whose names will go down as having played mighty roles in that page—the great page of our modern history.

---

[48] This is likely an error in the transcription, and the date should be 1776, a reference to the American Revolution, an event Nearing will return to later in his closing.

I'd like to tell you something further. I said that socialism was progressive as well as capitalism. Now you think over here, because of what you read in the New York Times, that the Russian Revolution is not very popular perhaps in Europe. I want to tell you that you cannot go in Europe today, even in the mercenary little countries built up around Russia by the treaty, you cannot go in and raise a real respectable army of working men to fight against Russia—(applause)—because now—I have only two more minutes—because the workers of Europe believe in Russia. (Applause.) The workers of Italy have started to make their revolution. The workers all over Central Europe have started to make their revolution. There is not a country of any considerable size in Europe where the workers are not today busy preparing the foundations of the new socialist state.

Is Russian liberty, says Professor Seligman, symptomatic of liberty in general? No. Civil war, blockades, all of the horrors that we have added to their period of transformation, all of those things are non-symptomatic of socialism in general. But in Russia they have taken over the resources, they have taken over transportation, machinery, they have taken over the factories, the community owns the means of its own livelihood. And they have appointed a Supreme Council of National Economy, and they are going to organize the nation as an economic unit on economic lines. It is the first time in history that it has ever been attempted. If it does not succeed in Russia it will succeed somewhere else, maybe here, because that is symptomatic of socialism—the application of modern organized intelligence to the problem of getting a living. (Prolonged applause.)

Analysis of Negative Rebuttal

It appears that none of Seligman's arguments caught Nearing off-guard. He had solid, relatable rebuttals to each key argument.

The benefits ascribed to capitalism, in terms of increased prosperity, ought to be assigned, instead, to the Industrial Revolution, to the progress of technology that comes to all. Surely, railroads exist under socialism as well.

Nearing then argues that capitalism is indeed progressive, but not in the way Seligman suggests. Instead, it is the intensification of capital in production—the requirement for more, bigger, and costlier machinery—that is progressive, and this prevents workers from starting their own businesses and forces them into factory employment.

This seems like a weak argument, even for 1921. Did Ford, Carnegie, the Wright Brothers, Marconi, or Edison start off with large capital investments and huge factories?

Nearing then, in what must have been prepared remarks, quotes extensively from Seligman's 1915 pamphlet "An Economic Interpretation of the War," where Seligman had proposed a model of historical economic development, where first there was competition among nations for wealth in the form of raw materials, then for markets to sell finished goods, and finally competition for markets for capital, i.e., for lending funds. Seligman argued that World War I was an example of this third phase, where Germany and England vied for access to the world's markets.

Although Nearing quotes Seligman's text, he makes the opposite conclusion. Seligman, in that pamphlet, argued that the conflict would resolve itself, leading to an optimistic outcome when industrialization comes to all nations, and at that point the exploitation of underdeveloped nations would cease, as well as economic conflict among nations:

> Then, and then only, will Adam Smith's dream be realized, namely, that each nation will be able to utilize its own climatic and other economic advantages in a peaceful struggle with other nations. Then, and then only, will universal free trade become profitable to all, and the rule of international amity become enduring. Then, and then only, shall we have the secure foundation laid for the world republic and for the cooperation of all races and of all peoples toward a common ideal.

Nearing invokes Seligman's conflict model, but finds not resolution, but progressive "starvation, industrial slavery, war."

Nearing then goes into an extensive invocation of the struggles of the Russian people, first against the Czar, and then against an alliance of White Russian reactionaries and blockading Western imperialist powers. It is this opposition, the prolonged birth pangs, and the novelty of their new order, that explains current suffering in Russia. In this Nearing echoes the remarks of Villard in his introductory remarks, that this is social experimentation.

Affirmative Conclusion (Seligman)

Villard: Ladies and Gentlemen: This is the third and last round. (Laughter.) Professor Seligman leads off.

~

Mr. Nearing tells us that Messrs. Lenin and Trotsky have been true to the old adage—"He who shall not work, neither shall he eat"—a noble sentiment. My interpretation of what Messrs. Lenin and Trotsky are doing would be this—"He who shall work or not, he shall not eat." (Slight applause.) That is what is happening in Russia today and it is not due to the blockade, it is not due simply to the results of the war, because the conditions are getting worse and worse, because Russia has been able to live on the results of the past accumulation of capitalism. Socialism is bringing about a situation, the most horrible, the most frightful, the most hideous that the world has ever seen—the disappearance of culture, the disappearance of cities, the disappearance of civilization, and the rapid progression of universal starvation among the workers themselves. That is socialism in practice.

Now, ladies and gentlemen, in the few minutes that are left I want to make the point that my respected antagonist has not met the arguments, weak arguments though they be, which I have attempted to put forward. He has not shown that the capitalist and the recipient of private interest, rent, and profits—he has not shown that such a man does not contribute and contribute largely to the result, and that his disappearance will mean a diminution of production and, therefore, an increase of misery. He has not disproved in the second place, the point that I made at the beginning, that ever since 1873 our panics, and what he calls the intermittent starvation, have become less and less owing to the integration and development of capitalism itself. He must meet that point in order to win his case as an argument. In the third place, he has not shown that all the beautiful results, desirable as they are, which he thinks can alone be achieved by socialism, cannot be accomplished under what I would call progressive capitalism.

My program of social reform is this. I will put it shortly under these seven heads, and not one of them needs socialism: equality of opportunity through increase of education and the disappearance of unjust privileges; second, the raising of the level of competition by law and public opinion; third, increasing the participation in industry through what is called "industrial democracy"[49] and what is rapidly going on under representative government today; fourth, diminution of the instability of employment through the application of the principle of insurance which we have already applied to accidents

---

[49] Which is to say, trade unionism and collective bargaining. *Industrial Democracy* was an influential book by British socialists Sidney and Beatrice Webb, published in 1897.

and which we are beginning to apply elsewhere; fifth, conservation of national resources in order to prevent the waste which is responsible for much of the present-day trouble; sixth, social control of potential monopoly which has been proceeding apace and which has even reached unheard of lengths in some modern countries; finally the resumption for the community of swollen and unduly large fortunes through the use of taxation which must go, however, only to that point of not stifling and killing the spirit of enterprise which socialism would bring about. (Applause.)

Now, ladies and gentlemen, every one of these points is what I call a mark of progressive capitalism and not one of them needs socialism. Socialism is a beautiful theory, although the theorists are fighting among each other, as they did yesterday in France and the day before in Italy. Lenin and Trotsky don't agree with each other and few other socialists would agree with either. But the practical point is that when socialism is put into operation it liberates certain forces which automatically reduce the production of wealth, and which when pushed to their utmost extreme, will gradually undo the chief work that civilization has accomplished.

I maintain, ladies and gentlemen, that socialism is not practicable, because it misconceives the real nature of human beings, that it is not desirable because it will ultimately land us in a tyranny, or if it be not a tyranny then in an unspeakable inefficiency. And I maintain that socialism is not inevitable because it is based upon a misunderstanding of the real forces, the ultimate forces, the progressive forces that are at work under capitalism.

Let us not forget, ladies and gentlemen, that our modern civilization, imperfect though it be, has been the result of a piecemeal and laborious upbuilding, and that it is not the mark of either wisdom or statesmanship to think that it can be rebuilt at once. Let us not throw away the fruits of all modern achievements and take a leap in the dark which may land us in the abyss of impotence. I claim, ladies and gentlemen, that what we need is the patience, the wise and large patience that is born of long experience and of ripe wisdom. We must remember that nothing in the world has ever been built up simply by bitterness and by negation, and that if we create anything at all we must build not on the shifting sands of an unreal and untrue psychology of human nature, but that we must build on the solid foundation of actual fact. It is much easier to promise a new heaven and a new Earth than to set resolutely to work and improve that little bit of our Earth which is nearest to us. We do indeed, ladies and gentlemen, need idealism. But we want an idealism that is tempered with moderation and that is transfused with practicability. If we are idealists in this sense, then, and then alone, I claim we can look forward to a future of industrial society which will preserve the old, while gaining the new, and which will show that it is pregnant with the seeds of real progress, ever renewing itself and ultimately achieving the much desired harmony and social justice. (Great applause.)

Analysis of Affirmative Conclusion

Seligman quickly attacks the assertion that present difficulties in Russia are due to the Russian Civil War and the Western blockade. How could this be, if conditions are getting worse, not better over time? (Allied powers withdrew in 1920.) Seligman argues that what we're seeing is Russia depleting their previously accumulated capital and their socialist economy is unable to keep the people from starvation.

He then frames the debate and claims that Nearing must successfully argue three points to win the debate: 1) That capitalists do not substantially contribute to prosperity and therefore do not deserve their rent, profits, etc., 2) That financial panics have not diminished in frequency as capitalism as progressed, and 3) That the benefits Nearing claims for socialism cannot also be obtained by "progressive capitalism."

Of course, from our vantage point, post Great Depression, Seligman's claim about reduced financial panics is cringeworthy. But this does not mean Nearing is right. They are both wrong. They have both misdiagnosed the causes of financial panics.

Seligman then outlines a program of social reform, which he claims would address Nearing's concerns, but within a capitalist system, e.g., trade unionism, unemployment insurance, anti-trust enforcement, increased taxation on the wealthy, etc. This is pretty much a litany of Progressive-era ideas which would be implemented a decade later in the New Deal.

Seligman finally reverses Nearing's argument that we should take a wait-and-see attitude with socialism and not to judge it too harshly until we've worked through the kinks in the system. Seligman argues, on the contrary, we should be patient with capitalism, and build it up rather than tear it down and start anew. He argues that socialism is a false ideology, born of bitterness and based on a false psychology.

Negative Conclusion (Nearing)

Villard: Mr. Nearing has the last word. (Applause.)

∼

There is one point of fact that I should like to clear up, if I can, and that is about the intensity of panics. In the panic of 1873: the largest number of failures in 1873 was 5,183 failures; 1893: the largest number of failures in 1893 was 15,242, or three times the number for 1873. We come on down to the next great panic, 1913, when the total number of commercial failures was 22,156, or 50% more than those of the preceding panic.

(A Lady: How about the proportions?)

Nearing: Yes, there is something in that. You would compare that with the population and the total volume of business.

Now, I want to speak another word of fact. Professor Seligman says that the situation in Russia is bad. Yes, I'd like to read him a sentence or two from the January letter of the National City Bank, the largest in the Americas:

"The second year following the Armistice did not bring the degree of industrial recovery and social recuperation among the peoples of Europe which had been hoped for. Conditions over the greater part of the continent are still in great confusion, and over much of it even more distressing than a year ago."

"Poland. The industrial and financial situation is very bad, with the currency depreciated almost to the vanishing point by the enormous issues of the past year"— all over Europe, this thing that is harming Russia—in Poland conditions are deplorable. There is no socialism on the surface in Poland. (Applause.) What is the trouble with Europe? Why she has just spent twenty-five millions of wealth on a grand jamboree called the World War, and she has not come through the result. She has not come through the after-effects. Europe is suffering a war, not socialism. Russia has had six years of war, and she is suffering a war like the rest of Europe. Give Russia and the other socialist countries of Europe—well, be generous with them—give them twenty years. You remember how long it took us to come out of our four years of Civil War? Give Russia twenty years and the other countries of Europe twenty years before passing final judgement. (Great applause.)

Really, however, the issue between Professor Seligman and myself is very simple. He don't think the people can handle their own economic affairs, and I do. (Laughter.) Back in 1776 they told the American people that they could not handle their own political affairs, and the American people went ahead and tried it anyway. (Laughter.) Well, they have not done a 100% job. (Hearty laughter.) But then, on the whole, the result has been better than if we had let George III and his descendants do the job for us.

(Applause.) I don't mean that the workers anywhere in the world can do a 100% job in handling their economic lives, but I do mean this, that people learn by trying.

That is the great thing about the Russian Revolution. You look at the failures of Russia, but you don't go into a laboratory where chemists are working and say, "Show me your latest failure." (Laughter.) I could take any newspaper man in the hall into the Edison laboratory down here to Orange,[50] and I could show him enough failures to write a full-page story that would show the Edison laboratory up as the worst calamity in New Jersey. (Laughter and applause.) It is not because people fail. It is because they don't try.

That is the trouble with the people of America. What was it that we admired about our ancestors? Was it because they succeeded? No, because they had the nerve to stand up and try for themselves. (Great applause.) And that is what we admire today about the people of Russia. Of all the people of Europe, when this catastrophe struck them, they struggled out from under it, got on their feet a little bit and started out to try for themselves. Now, that is an example that has thrilled the world. This doesn't have to succeed. They don't have to make good a single one of their endeavors. Just to have tried when everybody else was failing—that was something. (Applause.)

---

[50] Now a National Historical Site, Edison's laboratory and his home, Glenmont, were in West Orange, New Jersey.

And that is what Russia did. She tried. And that is what I want to see the workers of the United States do. I want to see them try. (Great applause.) Professor Seligman thinks we can tinker up the old machine. (Hearty laughter.) I believe that no house divided against itself can stand. Where you get a country split, as our country is split, between men who live without working, on the labor of others, and great masses who labor when they get a chance and get only part of the product of their work, when you get that kind of a fundamental economic division, you have begun to build classes and that country will never again be at peace until that economic division is ironed out. There are two things before us: one to be a plutocracy where wealth rules absolutely, and where men and women are stepped on like the dirt of the street; and the other is to set up self-government [in] economic life where men and women handle their own economic affairs just as now they try to handle their own political affairs. Professor Seligman wants to see the plutocracy progress a little further. I'd like to see a bit of the socialism showing its head here and there now. (Prolonged applause.)

Analysis of Negative Conclusion

Nearing begins by rattling off statistics on corporate failures by year, attempting to contradict Seligman by showing that failures are increasing, not decreasing. But he quickly drops the issue when he is called out by a woman in the audience who points out that he has failed to normalize the counts by the changing size of the economy.

Nearing then addresses Seligman's claim that the economy in Russian remains in ruins and is getting worse. Nearing quotes from a bank annual report to make the point that situation in other war-torn but non-communist countries are in bad shape as well. The cause, claims Nearing, is a slow recovery from the war, and has nothing to do with socialism. We should reserve judgement, he suggests, for twenty years.

Nearing then launches into his peroration, saying that just as Americans tinkered with political systems at our Founding, and continue to tinker with technology as Edison does, and although we sometimes fail when trying, over time we tend to succeed, and so (gosh darn) it is also so very American to tinker with economic systems as well. In this sense he again echoes Villard, the debate's chairman.

Known to us now, but not to Nearing in 1921, Lenin would just three months later retreat from his disastrous socialist economic program and move to a mixed-economy, re-introducing free market and profit elements, in what was termed the "New Economic Policy." So much for tinkering with socialism.

Finally, Nearing claims that tinkering with capitalism will not work because there is an irreconcilable gulf between the owner and the worker, a class struggle, a conflict between plutocracy and economic self-government.

Who Won the Debate?

To a modern reader it is notable how skewed to the left the debate was. Nearing made the orthodox Marxist argument: exploitation of the worker, alienation, greedy bankers, and parasitic capitalists, etc. He argued for flat out nationalization of industry and the elimination of private property in the means of production. He wanted a revolution, in America, akin to that in Russia.

Seligman, ostensibly the defender of capitalism in this debate, agreed that capitalism, as it existed in the real world, was indeed flawed, but that it was progressive, in the sense that it gradually improved, and that via wealth redistribution and an enlarged social welfare system with social insurance, it could be made tolerable to workers.

No one in this debate argued free markets in the classical liberal or laissez-faire sense. This was a debate between a progressive social democrat and a socialist. In contemporary terms, this was a debate between Elizabeth Warren and a young Bernie Sanders.

Seligman had the harder task in this debate. The person defending capitalism has a handicap, in that he must defend a system at work in an imperfect and corrupt world, while the socialist can argue optimistic ideals at play in an imaginary world.

Rhetorically, Seligman showed masterful rhetoric in his prepared remarks, especially his closing. He did less well on impromptu rebuttals. Nearing was more effective in relating his comments to the workingmen in the largely friendly audience, although his argument stands up less well to scrutiny.

Contemporary opinion of the debate (discussed in the next chapter) called it a draw. However, in the long-term Seligman's views won out in America, and lead, through the New Deal, to welfare capitalism in this country, rather than to outright socialism.

Reactions and Recollections

The immediate newspaper coverage, the day after in the *New York Herald*, called it a draw:

> [A]t the end the Socialist majority was just as vehement and the capitalist minority was just as spirited and neither speaker had convinced the other that his system was wrong.

(The complete review can be found in Appendix C.)

The Fine Arts Guild (the debate sponsors) quickly published a volume based on a stenographic transcription of the debate and declared it, in their advertisements, to be "The Greatest Debate in a Decade!"

However, historian David Saville Muzzey, reviewing the published transcript of the debate (see Appendix D), was underwhelmed:

> In the end the debate came to the conclusion which a man without great prophetic insight might have predicted—an irreconcilable difference in points of view, the conservative versus the radical. As an exhibition of forensic courtesy, the debate was all that could be desired. As a penetrating and sympathetic analysis, appreciation and refutation

of the adversary's arguments, it left much to be desired.

Of course, it is worth considering the possibility that neither side was aiming to change opinions. It is quite possible that both recognized that the debate had attracted a highly polarized audience, and so each debater focused on appealing to their own base, using the occasion to instruct their adherents in the best current arguments rather than convert their opponent's followers.

Seligman and Nearing would meet once again at the Mecca Temple (now called the New York City Center) on February 2, 1930 for a three-way debate on the question, "Whether capitalism offers more to the workers of the world than socialism or communism." Seligman, then nearly 70 years old, defended capitalism against Nearing, arguing for communism, and Fenner Brockway,[51] arguing for socialism.

From contemporary reactions, this 1930 debate appeared to have been before a far more raucous audience than previous ones, with speakers, especially Seligman, being shouted down by cries of "Lies! Lies!" when reporting on conditions in the Soviet Union.[52]

---

[51] Fenner Brockway (1888–1988), British socialist and Member of Parliament. During the Spanish Civil War he helped recruit British volunteers, including Eric Blair (George Orwell).

[52] Harry Engelman, "Communist Tolerance," *The Tablet* (Brooklyn, N.Y.), 15 February 1930, p. 6.

Many years later, in his autobiography, Nearing recalled his encounter with Prof. Seligman, with an odd mix of respect and disdain:

> The shrewdest defender of capitalism with whom I had an opportunity to debate was Professor E.R.A. Seligman...Professor Seligman's position at Columbia commanded respect. His presence on the platform was proof of his commitment to capitalism. He had a fine platform manner, spoke fluently, urbanely. He had an impressive beard and was always immaculately and stylishly dressed. He was perhaps thirty years my senior. He was a perfect example of the shrewd apologist for the status quo.[53]

---

[53] Scott Nearing, *The Making of a Radical: A Political Autobiography* (White River Junction, Vt.: Chelsea Green Publishing Co., 2000)

What did Mises see?

So, what is it that Mises saw in this cheaply printed transcript of a New York City music hall debate? What about it led Mises to commend it as "instructive" and include it in the appendix to his 1927 book, *Liberalism*? As we've seen, Seligman did not score a knock-out victory for the capitalist argument. By all accounts, few minds were changed at the time.

I think it is worth noting that Mises was a polymath. He did not confine himself narrowly to economics His thinking ranged more broadly, over economics, politics, philosophy, history, psychology, etc.

I suspect Mises might have found sympathy with his own thoughts in these debate remarks by Seligman:

> Socialism is bringing about a situation, the most horrible, the most frightful, the most hideous that the world has ever seen—the disappearance of culture, the disappearance of cities, the disappearance of civilization, and the rapid progression of universal starvation among the workers themselves. That is socialism in practice.

Mises would have liked that. He shared the belief that private property was key to civilization, prosperity, and world peace, as well as the fear that socialism was an unmitigated disaster:

> Everywhere today political power is in the hands of the antiliberal parties. The program of antiliberalism unleashed the forces that gave rise to the great World War and, by virtue of import and export quotas, tariffs, migration barriers, and similar measures, has brought the nations of the world to the point of mutual isolation. Within each nation it has led to socialist experiments whose result has been a reduction in the productivity of labor and a concomitant increase in want and misery. Whoever does not deliberately close his eyes to the facts must recognize everywhere the signs of an approaching catastrophe in world economy. Antiliberalism is heading toward a general collapse of civilization.—*Liberalism*, p.2

Appendix A

Newspaper coverage of an earlier debate between Seligman and Nearing on the topic of academic freedom. From the *Times Union* (Brooklyn), 17 March 1917, p. 3

SCOTT NEARING
STIRS DEBATE
CALLS UNIVERSITY PROFESSORS WORSE THAN MERCENARY AT ACADEMY DISCUSSION

Four national authorities on education appeared in debate under the auspices of the Brooklyn Institute at the Academy of Music last night on the question, "Have Our Universities Academic Freedom?"

Edwin R.A. Seligman of Columbia, and T.S. Adams, of Yale, spoke for the affirmative, while Scott Nearing, who was forced out of Pennsylvania University last year and resigned under criticism from Toledo University last week, and Willard C. Fisher, of New York, argued in the negative.

Prof. Nearing, as was expected, furnished the feature of the evening by a comprehensive assault on the university educational system and a scathing denunciation of the principles of the teaching staffs.

Prof. Nearing quoted the definition of academic freedom from Nicholas Murray Butler, of Columbia, that academic freedom means the right of search for truth irrespective of religious, political and social relationship.

"A man should have the right to state what his conscience dictates to him is right, either inside or outside of the classroom, but this right is denied him in our universities to-day. He is compelled to stick in the same old path, that is, in a rut. Of course, a professor may go out of his field in some subject without fear of disapproval. He may delve in Egyptian, Babylonian, Assyrian, or Etruscan antiquity without risk of consequences, or he may wander into the realms of astronomy with impunity and have no fear of contradiction. Why is a man free in these domains and not free in working out some economic alignment? As long as a man deals with the past he is safe, but when he essays to stir up the present, when he has the temerity and courage to upset the plutocratic apple cart, then he must look out for unpleasant results."

"The instructional staff in our State and miscellaneous universities are not free but tied hand and foot by trustee government, holding big interests. They want to keep a young man on their own track, in the rut, as I have said. They get him when young and they train him in the conservative way they ant him to go. The majority of men and women teachers are those who specialize in philosophy, ethics and kindred subjects and must conform to the old routine; they do not teach what they believe; they dare not teach what they believe; they are slackers, quitters, loafers."

Prof. Nearing thundered the denunciation with all the fiery eloquence of which he is master.

"When they encroach on a field which threatens the established order," he went on, "their jobs are in danger. A man's job is at stake if he says anything to distort the present social order. The problem is a bread-and-butter problem, the teacher must live and he has been trained and brought up in only one direction, to make a livelihood, so, like the shoe-maker, he must stick to his last and stifle his own conscience, repress what he knows to be right and knuckle under to the powers above him. He is dwarfed, stunted, seared, withered, but for the sake of a living he can only grin and bear it."

"Many a man does not like his job, but circumstances compel him to stick to it, There are many engaged in the manufacture of munitions who loathe and abhor war, but their work is a necessity to themselves and families, and they are powerless to help themselves. So it is with the teachers."

Prof. Seligman scored Prof. Nearing for applying to college professors a term descriptive of women of the streets.

"I want nothing to do with a man who uses such a phrase," retorted Prof. Seligman, "he has no right to demand recognition from any well-meaning individual in this community."

In reply to a question from an individual in the audience, Prof. Nearing strongly denounced the Rockefeller and Carnegie Foundations.

"No private individual has a right," he contended, "to subsidize an educational establishment in a democracy like ours, his interference is subversive of the best interests of the republic."

Prof. Seligman said that the topic assigned was as old as civilization, and that freedom of speech and action depended upon environment and the laws governing educational institutions. He pointed out that in the Middle Ages, in which universities had origin, they became the bulwarks against oppression and boldly stood forth for freedom."

He cited how Paris University in the fourteenth century made a fight against Pope and King, and took sharp issues on the questions of dogma and doctrine.

"Ever since," continued the professor, "the university has been the home of freedom, but of course, there have been many changes. Often these seats of learning succeeded, but when democracy was receding and when political absolutism got in the ascendant the universities lost the fight. Here in America we have had ups and downs. We have gone through an evolution, but conditions are inevitable making for a broader recognition of academic freedom.

"In this country thee earlier institutions of learning were not universities, thy were academies and high schools, which gradually developed into colleges, nearly all, however, under the sheltering wings of some religious body and naturally they became tinged and flavored with certain religious beliefs. Many of them were proprietary institutions endowed by men whose ideas they were compelled to propagate.

"In these there was not freedom, because any man who accepted a professorship had to teach what the founder or patron wished to be taught. Yet, out of these proprietary schools evolved the colleges which gradually threw off the shackles of individual domination.

"But freedom necessitates responsibility and often the responsibility which attaches to freedom is neglected; there are two forms of responsibility, that of the classroom and of the outside. My whole point is this—just as there is a necessity for academic freedom so there is an equal need for academic responsibility. I believe that tin the great institutions of this country there is no restraint."

Prof. Adams supported the affirmative side, though he admitted that a professor or instructor of conservative ideas and principles had a better opportunity and chance than one of a radical or socialist tendency.

Prof. Willard Fisher declared for the negative in a humorous address. It would not be tactical, he said, for a professor to attack child labor if one of the trustees owned a mill in which poor little starving children with stunted bodies were employed to help add to the wealth of the owner.

Appendix B

Another news store on the 1917 debate encounter between Seligman and Nearing. From the *Carbondale Daily News* (Carbondalte, Pa.) 17 March 1917, p. 7

∽

DR. SCOTT NEARING
ENLIVENS DEBATE

Declares That University Professors Teach What They Do Not Believe—Dr. Seligman Replies.

New York, March 17.—Things were going along rather smoothly in the forum debate held in the music hall of the Academy of Music, Brooklyn, last night, under the auspices of the Brooklyn institute of Arts and Sciences, when Professor Scott Nearing, formerly of the University of Pennsylvania, but now of Toledo University, caused a stir among the one thousand persons assembled by declaring, "I know scores of university professors who teach what they do not believe, and I want to say that the man who teaches something he doesn't believe is prostituting his intellect."

Professor Nearing was arrayed with Professor Willard C. Fisher, of the New York University, on the negative side of the question. "Have American Universities Academic Freedom?" Professor Edwin R. A. Seligman, of Columbia

University, and Professor T. S. Adams, of Yale University, spoke on the affirmative side of the debate.

Professor Seligman declared there never had been any deliberate attempt to limit the freedom of thought and expression of university professors and had seemingly made out a very clear case for the affirmative when Dr. Nearing took the rostrum.

"If any university professor dared to teach what he believes, and if what he believes is contrary to the economic interests of the university that employs him," declared Professor Nearing, near the close of his speech. "he would be speedily dismissed." Then he emphasized his contention with the first statement quoted.

Professor Seligman immediately jumped to his feet, and in rebuttal angrily said; "I want to publicly state that I will have nothing to do with any man who would arraign his colleagues as Professor Nearing has arraigned them tonight. And furthermore, any professor who makes such a statement has no right to demand recognition in any university in this country."

Professor Seligman's retort was received with much handclapping, but a few hisses from the centre of the audience indicated Professor Nearing was not alone in his views.

Appendix C

Coverage of the 1921 capitalism versus socialism debate, as printed on page 15 of the 24 January 1921 issue of the *New York Herald*.

∼

CAPITAL DEFENDED BY PROF. SELIGMAN

Columbia University Economist Engages in Debate With Scott Nearing.

AUDIENCE TAKES SIDES

Socialists in Majority, but Neither Speaker Succeeds in Convincing the Other.

Socialism, as personified by Scott Nearing, and Capitalism, with Prof. R. A. Seligman as its champion, locked horns in a three hour grapple yesterday afternoon in the Lexington Theatre before an audience which overflowed the big building. At the beginning of the argument the Socialist majority in the audience applauded their orator vehemently and the capitalist minority applauded their spokesman most spiritedly. And at the end the Socialist majority was just as vehement and the capitalist minority was just as spirited and neither speaker had convinced the other that his system was wrong.

The debate, which was arranged by the Fine Arts Guild, was remarkable in several ways, not the least of which was the number of persons who literally enacted a mob scene in the lobby in an effort to get tickets at regular theatre rates to hear the debate. Many of these had come from Boston, Philadelphia and other cities to hear this verbal combat between Prof. Seligman of conservatIve Columbia, one of the best known authorities on economics in this country, and Scott Nearing of the radical Rand School of Social Science, one of the country's most emphatic Socialists. Nearing, although not so restrained in his utterances as Prof. Seligman, was not so startling in his utterances as during the war.

Audience With Nearing

It was plain from the start that Prof. Seligman was on hostile territory. The weight of applause was decidedly against him: some of his remarks were greeted with laughter, and at least one man or woman booed him during a burst of applause; he spoke first, while Mr. Nearing had the cleanup position; he was on the drafty side of the house and was compelled to wrap an overcoat around himself during his rest periods in the engagement: the assistant chairman was polite to him and moved his table to the front for him while Scott Nearing moved his own; Oswald Garrison Villard, who presided, said kind words concerning Socialism, though none concerning capitalism, and, as Prof. Seligman pointed out in the course of his address, he

The Great Seligman-Nearing Debate of 1921

was defending an actual condition, while Mr. Nearing was advocating a beautiful theory.

"It's much easier to promise a new heaven and new Earth than it is to set to work to improve that little bit of the Earth which is nearest to us," he said, in concluding his summary.

The debate was on the subject: Resolved, that capitalism has more to offer to the workers of the United States than has socialism.

Mr. Villard, In his opening remarks announced that he was a middle of the road man, with leanings toward neither system.

Prof. Seligman devoted his first period largely to defining the terms and explaining the capitalist system, showing that it was progressive and based on democracy and freely admitting its weaknesses, which, he said, would be eliminated by the progress of the system itself. He stated that there is no reason why workmen should be forced to bear the burden of unemployment, but pointed out that tentative steps are being taken here and elsewhere to remedy this condition. The "joylessness" of the workmen, he pointed out, is due not to capitalism but to the monotony of tending machines, and machines must be tended under any system. Capitalism is still virtually in its infancy, he said, and will grow and improve with the years.

Capitalism and Undernourishment

Mr. Nearing plunged boldly into his argument. "Under the capitalist system the worker has to expect intermittent starvation, slavery and war," he asserted. "In this, the richest of countries, and in this city, the center of wealth, we reported oven before the last economic unpleasantness 26% of our school children undernourished."

He charged that the Federal Reserve System was privately "owned." and asserted that children were "pumped full of virulent propaganda for the present not capitalist system."

"A shot is fired in the Balkans and the 10,000,000 men go to their graves to decide that Britain shall hold Bagdad, gateway to the East, and that Germany shall pay what she can," he asserted, in an effort to prove the last conflict was due to capitalism. He summed up Socialism as giving the workers subsistence, economic government and a basis for peace.

Prof. Seligman thrust oratorical pins into the Socialist belief, as advanced by Mr. Nearing, that the capitalist can get along without the workman and can drop him at will and without damage to his own welfare. He read official documents from Russia in which the workers of Petrograd complained they were being treated as slaves, that strikers were being shot, and the strictest discipline and fines were exacted in the factories.

"Socialism starts out with beautiful ideals and ends with tyranny to prevent starvation," he said. "I don't deny there is some theft, some robbery in capitalism, but I do say the essence of capitalism, the essence of profits, is service. People can't in the lone run make great profits unless they really give service to the community."

Mr. Nearing asserted that the same forces that swept the world into war in 1914 were moving to precipitate another conflict between the United States and Britain and Japan. He asserted that all over Europe the workers are moving toward solidarity, and that there is not a country in Europe where the workers are not already preparing the foundations for a new Socialist state. He praised Russia for trying to form a new state while harassed by war and famine.

"That's what Russia did. She tried." he said. "and that's what I want to see the United States do. I want to see them try."

Appendix D

David Saville Muzzey's[54] review of the published transcript of the 1921 debate was printed in *The Standard*, Vol VII, No. 7, March 1921.

∼

"The Seligman-Nearing Debate"

We have in hand the stenographic report of the joint debate held in the Lexington Avenue Opera House, on the afternoon of January 23rd, between Professor Edwin R. A. Seligman and Professor Scott Nearing, on the subject: "Resolved, that Capitalism has more to offer Labor than Socialism." Mr. Oswald Garrison Villard presided and in his felicitous introductory remarks made a plea for greater willingness on the part of Americans to hear and discuss opinions contrary to those which they have come to believe right. From the tone of the Chairman's remarks, asking a fair hearing for Socialism, one would judge that the huge audience represented the "bourgeois" class. And the price of the tickets would go far to confirm that judgment.

Professor Seligman, who supported the affirmative, led off. He called attention to the fact that while Capitalism

---

[54] David Saville Muzzey (1870-1965) was an American historian and textbook author.

is an established system with many generations of experience, Socialism, except for sporadic experiments in the middle of the Nineteenth century "and the gigantic enterprise that is now being conducted by Soviet Russia," is a theory. The discussion, therefore, must deal with the known and the trried on one side, and with conjectures and prophecies on the other. Moreover, there is great divergence in the views of the Socialists themselves—the anarchistic, the collectivist, the sentimental, the scientific, the Syndicalist, and the Guild Socialist. Karl Marx, the high priest of Socialism, is not followed today in all points of his doctrine; the poor are not growing poorer, but richer, as the rich grow richer; nor does Socialism grow towards the cataclysm in the countries in which Capitalism is most developed. It is in undeveloped, unenlightened Russia that the great Socialist revolution has come.

As the achievements of Capitalism which make for the greater welfare of the laborer, Professor Seligman cited: (1) the accumulation of wealth, making possible a cheapening of production and a multiplication of conveniences, comforts and even luxuries for the poor, which they could not have dreamed of a few generations ago; (2) the division of labor and the diversification of consumption, enabling the worker to draw on a great variety of producers for his food, clothing and other necessaries; (3) the democracy which has been called into being by the Industrial Revolution, which was made possible alone by Capitalism; and (4) the opportunities for education from the kindergarten up, which every capitalistic society has richly provided.

Professor Seligman did not deny that Capitalism has had "its weaknesses and excrescences": unfair competition, unjust privileges, and swollen fortunes. But he maintained that Capitalism was "progressive," that it had eliminated many of its worst faults and that it was on the way to eliminate more. In short, there was good ground for the expectation that the growing democracy in industry, the growing education in democracy, and the growing humanity in our society would purge out the cruelties that remain in Capitalism, and leave it with its positive and beneficial features alone—stability, order, competency, initiative,opportunity.

Professor Nearing was introduced by the Chairman as a man to whom "every American, whatever his economic beliefs, owes a debt of gratitude" for insisting "even in war-time upon that freedom of conscience and liberty to speak and write which are guaranteed by the Constitution of the United States"

It can hardly be said that Professor Nearing met, or endeavored to meet, the arguments of his opponent. Instead of answering the points which Professor Seligman made, he delivered an impassioned speech, punctuated by frequent outbursts of applause, and filled with striking statistics, to show the pitiable condition of the worker today. If Capitalism was "progressive," so were some diseases! Because the capitalist owns the machinery of production, the worker has to go to him and ask permission to work—or starve. "Prosperity, panic, and liquidation" is the recurring cycle of economic experience entailed by the capitalistic system. The United States is owned by a few capitalists. They say to the vast army of workers: Work and earn bread, and we will eat it! That is what Abraham Lincoln called slavery. Finally, Capitalism is responsible for war, with its overproduction of goods and its competition for markets. "In 1914 there was not a Socialist State in Europe... all the great group of capitalist Empires grabbing the world to rob it and fighting one another to death to determine who should do the plundering. They produced a surplus, as I said. They could not spend it at home. They took it abroad, and in the course of tak ing it abroad they had to make War—capitalistic War—and working men went and fought and died in that capitalistic War which they told us through their propaganda machinery was a War for Democracy. What does the worker want? Why he wants to keep the strings of economic life himself. Capitalism offers him intermittent starvation, industrial slavery, recurring war. Socialism offers him subsistence, economic self-government, a basis for peace."

In replying to this declamation, Professor Seligman pointed out that his opponent had not met his arguments, and that he had claimed for Socialism a Utopian program which the facts did not warrant. In the only instance where Socialism was tried on a large scale

(Soviet Russia) there was not intermittent but chronic starvation, not self-government but a detestable tyranny, not peace but massacres. He quoted Russian documents to show how the workers in that country protested that they were "hard-labor convicts," who had "become lost as human beings and turned into slaves." To which Professor Nearing in his rebuttal made the obvious answer that the reason for the tyranny in Russia was the intervention of the capitalistic states, including our own, which through invasion, blockade and boycott, thwarted the beneficient course which Lenine and Trotsky wished to pursue.

Except on the Russian question, which was a poor ground of debate, on account of the impossibility of the Socialist theory being applied in all honesty there, the two disputants did not lock horns. Rather, each made three speeches, fortifying his own theory, selecting facts and figures which were favorable to it alone. Each stated his position best, perhaps, in the final short summary. Professor Seligman main tained that the abolition of Capitalism in favor of an impracticable theory would mean a diminution of production and an increase of misery for the worker; that it would be to "throw away the fruits of all modem achievements and take a leap in the dark which might land us in the abyss of impotence." The sane method of socio-economic procedure was reform, not revolution. Education, industrial democracy, employers' insurance, conservation of resources, progressive taxation to abate the swollen fortunes—such were the means by which Capitalism (sound in its fundamentals) was to be purged of its abuses.

Professor Nearing rejected all these "palliatives." No amount of "tinkering with Capitalism" would cure its evils. The system itself is rotten at its foundations. "Really" he concluded, "the issue between Professor Seligman and myself is very simple. He doesn't think the people can handle their own economic affairs and I do." So in the end the debate came to the conclusion which a man without great prophetic insight might have predicted—an irreconcilable difference in points of view, the conservative versus the radical. As an exhibition of forensic courtesy, the debate was all that could be desired. As a penetrating and sympathetic analysis, appreciation and refutation of the adversary's arguments, it left much to be desired.

DAVID SAVILLE MUZZEY.

About the Author

Rob Weir studied astrophysics (Harvard College '91), then spent 27 years working in technology (IBM), and is now semi-retired, living in Dover, New Hampshire.

Weir writes on a range of topics, including political philosophy, history, and genealogy.

His libertarian blog is WhyNotLibertarianism.com.

Weir's annotated edition of Charle's Sprading's *Laconics of Liberty* is available in paperback and Kindle format at Amazon.

Weir can be emailed at rob@robweir.com

He can also be found on the following services:

> Blog: Twitter: @WhyNotLib
> Quora: https://www.quora.com/profile/Rob-Weir
> MeWe: @robcweir

www.ingramcontent.com/pod-product-compliance
Lightning Source LLC
Chambersburg PA
CBHW070944080526
44587CB00015B/2219